Macmillan McGraw

Math Connects

K

Lemonade 5¢

BEACH VACATIONS

Volume 1

Authors

Altieri • Balka • Day • Gonsalves • Grace • Krulik
Malloy • Molix-Bailey • Moseley • Mowry • Myren
Price • Reynosa • Santa Cruz • Silbey • Vielhaber

Macmillan/McGraw-Hill

About the Cover

Shapes, position, and patterns are featured topics in Kindergarten. Have students identify all of the shapes on the cover. Ask students to use words such as near/far to describe the position of the crab or the trees. Then have students describe the patterns they see on the cover.

The *McGraw-Hill* Companies

 Macmillan/McGraw-Hill

Send all inquiries to:
Macmillan/McGraw-Hill
8787 Orion Place
Columbus, OH 43240-4027

Volume 1
ISBN: 978-0-02-105723-8
MHID: 0-02-105723-0

Printed in the United States of America.

Math Connects, Grade K

6 7 8 9 10 RJE/LEH 16 15 14 13 12 11

Contents in Brief

Focal Points and Connections

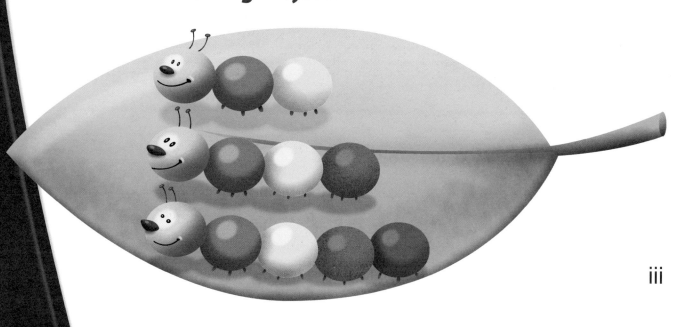

Focal Points

The Curriculum Focal Points identify key mathematical ideas for this grade. They are not discrete topics or a checklist to be mastered; rather, they provide a framework for the majority of instruction at a particular grade level and the foundation for future mathematics study. The complete document may be viewed at www.nctm.org/focalpoints.

KEY

GK-FP1
Grade K Focal Point 1

GK-FP2
Grade K Focal Point 2

GK-FP3
Grade K Focal Point 3

GK-FP4C
Grade K Focal Point 4
Connection

GK-FP5C
Grade K Focal Point 5
Connection

GK-FP6C
Grade K Focal Point 6
Connection

GK-FP1 *Number and Operations:* **Representing, comparing, and ordering whole numbers and joining and separating sets**

Children use numbers, including written numerals, to represent quantities and to solve quantitative problems, such as counting objects in a set, creating a set with a given number of objects, comparing and ordering sets or numerals by using both cardinal and ordinal meanings, and modeling simple joining and separating situations with objects. They choose, combine, and apply effective strategies for answering quantitative questions, including quickly recognizing the number in a small set, counting and producing sets of given sizes, counting the number in combined sets, and counting backward.

GK-FP2 *Geometry:* **Describing shapes and space**

Children interpret the physical world with geometric ideas (e.g., shape, orientation, spatial relations) and describe it with corresponding vocabulary. They identify, name, and describe a variety of shapes, such as squares, triangles, circles, rectangles, (regular) hexagons, and (isosceles) trapezoids presented in a variety of ways (e.g., with different sizes or orientations), as well as such three-dimensional shapes as spheres, cubes, and cylinders. They use basic shapes and spatial reasoning to model objects in their environment and to construct more complex shapes.

GK-FP3 *Measurement:* **Ordering objects by measurable attributes**

Children use measurable attributes, such as length or weight, to solve problems by comparing and ordering objects. They compare the lengths of two objects both directly (by comparing them with each other) and indirectly (by comparing both with a third object), and they order several objects according to length.

GK-FP4C *Data Analysis:* Children sort objects and use one or more attributes to solve problems. For example, they might sort solids that roll easily from those that do not. Or they might collect data and use counting to answer such questions as, "What is our favorite snack?" They re-sort objects by using new attributes (e.g., after sorting solids according to which ones roll, they might re-sort the solids according to which ones stack easily).

GK-FP5C *Geometry:* Children integrate their understandings of geometry, measurement, and number. For example, they understand, discuss, and create simple navigational directions (e.g., "Walk forward 10 steps, turn right, and walk forward 5 steps").

GK-FP6C *Algebra:* Children identify, duplicate, and extend simple number patterns and sequential and growing patterns (e.g., patterns made with shapes) as preparation for creating rules that describe relationships.

Reprinted with permission from *Curriculum Focal Points for Prekindergarten through Grade 8 Mathematics: A Quest for Coherence,* copyright 2006 by the National Council of Teachers of Mathematics. All rights reserved.

Authors

Mary Behr Altieri
Putnam/Northern
    Westchester BOCES
Yorktown Heights,
    New York

Don S. Balka
Professor Emeritus
Saint Mary's College
Notre Dame, Indiana

Roger Day, Ph.D.
Mathematics Department Chair
Pontiac Township High School
Pontiac, Illinois

Philip D. Gonsalves
Mathematics Coordinator
Alameda County Office
    of Education and
    California State
    University East Bay
Hayward, California

Ellen C. Grace
Consultant
Albuquerque,
    New Mexico

Stephen Krulik
Professor Emeritus
    Mathematics Education
Temple University
    Cherry Hill, New Jersey

Carol E. Malloy, Ph.D.
Associate Professor of
    Mathematics Education
University of North
    Carolina at Chapel Hill
Chapel Hill, North
    Carolina

Rhonda J. Molix-Bailey
Mathematics Consultant
Mathematics by Design
Desoto, Texas

Lois Gordon Moseley
Staff Developer
NUMBERS: Mathematics
    Professional
    Development
Houston, Texas

Brian Mowry
Independent Math Educational
    Consultant/Part-Time Pre-K
    Instructional Specialist
Austin Independent School District
Austin, Texas

Math Online Meet the Authors at macmillanmh.com

Christina L. Myren
Consultant Teacher
Conejo Valley Unified
    School District
Thousand Oaks, California

Jack Price
Professor Emeritus
California State
    Polytechnic University
Pomona, California

Mary Esther Reynosa
Instructional Specialist for
    Elementary Mathematics
Northside Independent
    School District
San Antonio, Texas

Rafaela M. Santa Cruz
SDSU/CGU Doctoral
    Program in Education
San Diego State University
San Diego, California

Robyn Silbey
Math Content Coach
Montgomery County
    Public Schools
Gaithersburg, Maryland

Kathleen Vielhaber
Mathematics Consultant
St. Louis, Missouri

Contributing Authors

Donna J. Long
Mathematics Consultant
Indianapolis, Indiana

FOLDABLES **Dinah Zike**
Educational Consultant
Dinah-Might Activities, Inc.
San Antonio, Texas

Consultants

Macmillan/McGraw-Hill wishes to thank the following professionals for their feedback. They were instrumental in providing valuable input toward the development of this program in these specific areas.

Mathematical Content

Viken Hovsepian
Professor of Mathematics
Rio Hondo College
Whittier, California

Grant A. Fraser, Ph.D.
Professor of Mathematics
California State University, Los Angeles
Los Angeles, California

Arthur K. Wayman, Ph.D.
Professor of Mathematics Emeritus
California State University, Long Beach
Long Beach, California

Assessment

Jane D. Gawronski, Ph.D
Director of Assessment and Outreach
San Diego State University
San Diego, California

Cognitive Guided Instruction

Susan B. Empson, Ph.D
Associate Professor of Mathematics
  and Science Education
University of Texas at Austin
Austin, Texas

English Learners

Cheryl Avalos
Mathematics Consultant
Los Angeles County Office of Education, Retired
Hacienda Heights, California

Kathryn Heinze
Graduate School of Education
Hamline University
St. Paul, Minnesota

Family Involvement

Paul Giganti, Jr.
Mathematics Education Consultant
Albany, California

Literature

David M. Schwartz
Children's Author, Speaker, Storyteller
Oakland, California

Vertical Alignment

Berchie Holliday
National Educational Consultant
Silver Spring, Maryland

Deborah A. Hutchens, Ed.D.
Principal
Norfolk Highlands Elementary
Chesapeake, Virginia

Reviewers

Each Reviewer reviewed at least two chapters of the Student Edition, giving feedback and suggestions for improving the effectiveness of the mathematics instruction.

Ernestine D. Austin
Facilitating Teacher/Basic Skills Teacher
LORE School
Ewing, NJ

Susie Bellah
Kindergarten Teacher
Lakeland Elementary
Humble, TX

Megan Bennett
Elementary Math Coordinator
Hartford Public Schools
Hartford, CT

Susan T. Blankenship
5th Grade Teacher – Math
Stanford Elementary School
Stanford, KY

Wendy Buchanan
3rd Grade Teacher
The Classical Center at Vial
Garland, TX

Sandra Signorelli Coelho
Associate Director for Mathematics
PIMMS at Wesleyan University
Middletown, CT

Joanne DeMizio
Asst. Supt., Math and Science Curriculum
Archdiocese of New York
New York, NY

Anthony Dentino
Supervisor of Mathematics
Brick Township Schools
Brick, NJ

Lorrie L. Drennon
Math Teacher
Collins Middle School
Corsicana, TX

Ethel A. Edwards
Director of Curriculum and Instruction
Topeka Public Schools
Topeka, KS

Carolyn Elender
District Elementary Math Instructional
    Specialist
Pasadena ISD
Pasadena, TX

Monica Engel
Educator Second Grade
Pioneer Elementary School
Bolingbrook, IL

Anna Dahinden Flynn
Math Teacher
Coulson Tough K-6 Elementary
The Woodlands, TX

Brenda M. Foxx
Principal
University Park Elementary
University Park, MD

Katherine A. Frontier
Elementary Teacher
Laidlaw
Western Springs, IL

Susan J. Furphy
5th Grade Teacher
Nisley Elementary
Grand Jct., CO

Peter Gatz
Student Services Coordinator
Brooks Elementary
Aurora, IL

Amber Gregersen
Teacher – 2nd Grade
Nisley Elementary
Grand Junction, Colorado

Roberta Grindle
Math and Language Arts Academic
    Intervention Service Provider
Cumberland Head Elementary School
Plattsburgh, NY

Sr. Helen Lucille Habig, RSM
Assistant Superintendent/Mathematics
Archdiocese of Cincinnati
Cincinnati, Ohio

Holly L. Hepp
Math Facilitator
Barringer Academic Center
Charlotte, NC

Martha J. Hickman
2nd Grade Teacher
Dr. James Craik Elementary School
Pomfret, MD

Margie Hill
District Coordinating Teacher for
    Mathematics, K-12
Blue Valley USD 229
Overland Park, KS

Carol H. Joyce
5th Grade Teacher
Nathanael Greene Elementary
Liberty, NC

Stella K. Kostante
Curriculum Coach
Roosevelt Elementary
Pittsburgh, PA

Pamela Fleming Lowe
Fourth Grade eMINTS Teacher
O'Neal Elementary
Poplar Bluff, MO

Lauren May, NBCT
4th Grade Teacher
May Watts Elementary School
Naperville, IL

Lorraine Moore
Grade 3 Math Teacher
Cowpens Elementary School
Cowpens, SC

Shannon L. Moorehead
4th Grade Teacher
Centervile Elementary
Anderson, SC

Gina M. Musselman, M.Ed
Kindergarten Teacher
Padeo Verde Elementary
Peoria, AZ

Jen Neufeld
3rd Grade Teacher
Kendall
Naperville, IL

Cathie Osiecki
K-5 Mathematics Coordinator
Middletown Public Schools
Middletown, CT

Phyllis L. Pacilli
Elementary Education Teacher
Fullerton Elementary
Addison, IL

Cindy Pearson
4th/5th Grade Teacher
John D. Spicer Elementary
Haltom City, TX 76137

Herminio M. Planas
Mathematics Curriculum Specialist
Administrative Offices-Bridgeport Public
    Schools
Bridgeport, CT

Jo J. Puree
Educator
Lackamas Elementary
Yelm, WA

Teresa M. Reynolds
Third Grade Teacher
Forrest View Elementary
Everett, WA

Dr. John A. Rhodes
Director of Mathematics
Indian Prairie SD #204
Aurora, IL

Amy Romm
1st Grade Teacher
Starline Elementary
Lake Havasu, AZ

Delores M. Rushing
Numeracy Coach
Dept. of Academic Services-Mathematics
    Department
Washington, DC

Daniel L. Scudder
Mathematics/Technology Specialist
Boone Elementary
Houston, TX

Laura Seymour
Resource Teacher Leader –Elementary
    Math & Science, Retired
Dearborn Public Schools
Dearborn, MI

Petra Siprian
Teacher
Army Trail Elementary School
Addison, IL

Sandra Stein
K-5 Mathematics Consultant
St. Clair County Regional Educational
    Service Agency
Marysville, MI

Barb Stoflet
Curriculum Specialist
Roseville Area Schools
Roseville, MN

Kim Summers
Principal
Dynard Elementary
Chaptico, MD

Ann C. Teater
4th Grade Teacher
Lancaster Elementary
Lancaster, KY

Anne E. Tunney
Teacher
City of Erie School District
Erie, PA

Joylien Weathers
1st Grade Teacher
Mesa View Elementary
Grand Junction, CO

Christine F. Weiss
Third Grade Teacher
Robert C. Hill Elementary School
Romeoville, IL

Contents

Start Smart

Contents

CHAPTER 1

Compare and Sort Objects

Contents

CHAPTER 2

Use Numbers 0 to 5

Contents

Focal Points and Connections

GK-FP6C

Contents

CHAPTER 4

Use Numbers to 10

Contents

Focal Points and Connections

GK-FP4C

CHAPTER 5

Construct and Use Graphs

Contents

Focal Points and Connections

GK-FP1

CHAPTER
6

Use Numbers to 20

Contents

Focal Points and Connections

GK-FP3

CHAPTER 7

Compare Measurements

Contents

CHAPTER 8

Use Numbers Beyond 20

Contents

Focal Points and Connections

GK-FP3

CHAPTER
9

Use Time

Contents

Focal Points
and Connections

GK-FP2

CHAPTER
10 **Describe Geometric Figures**

Focal Points
and Connections

GK-FP1

CHAPTER
11

Model Addition

Contents

CHAPTER
12 Model Subtraction

Contents

Looking Ahead

Problem-Solving Projects

Contents

Student Handbook

Photo Credits

WorkMat 1: Story Mat

WorkMat 2: Two-Part Mat

WorkMat 3: Graphing Mat

WorkMat 4: Sorting Mat/T-CHART

WorkMat 5: Ten-Frame

WorkMat 6: Ten-Frames

WorkMat 7: Part-Part-Whole

WorkMat 8: Number Lines

Start Smart

Let's Review!

Children Celebrating Their Country

Name: _____

Did you Know?

The Spotted Salamander is South Carolina's state amphibian.

Directions: Circle the animal that is above the palmetto tree. Underline the animal that is next to the palmetto tree. Place an X on the animal that is below the palmetto tree.

Name: _____

Number and Operations

Did you Know?

The Monarch butterfly is the state insect of Illinois.

Monarch Butterfly

Directions: Draw a line to match each butterfly to a flower. Count each butterfly. Count each flower.

Directions: Draw a line to match the number of insects with the same number of flowers.

Name: _____

Miniature Golf Course

Did you Know?

The first miniature golf course in the United States was built in North Carolina.

①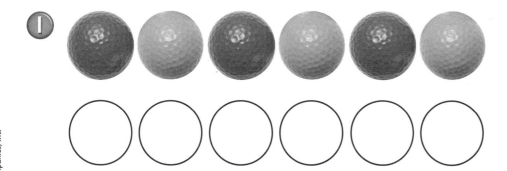

②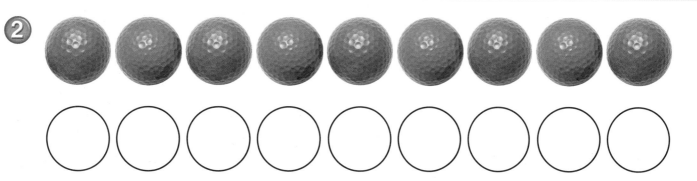

Directions 1–2: Identify each pattern. Copy the pattern by coloring the circles.

Start Smart

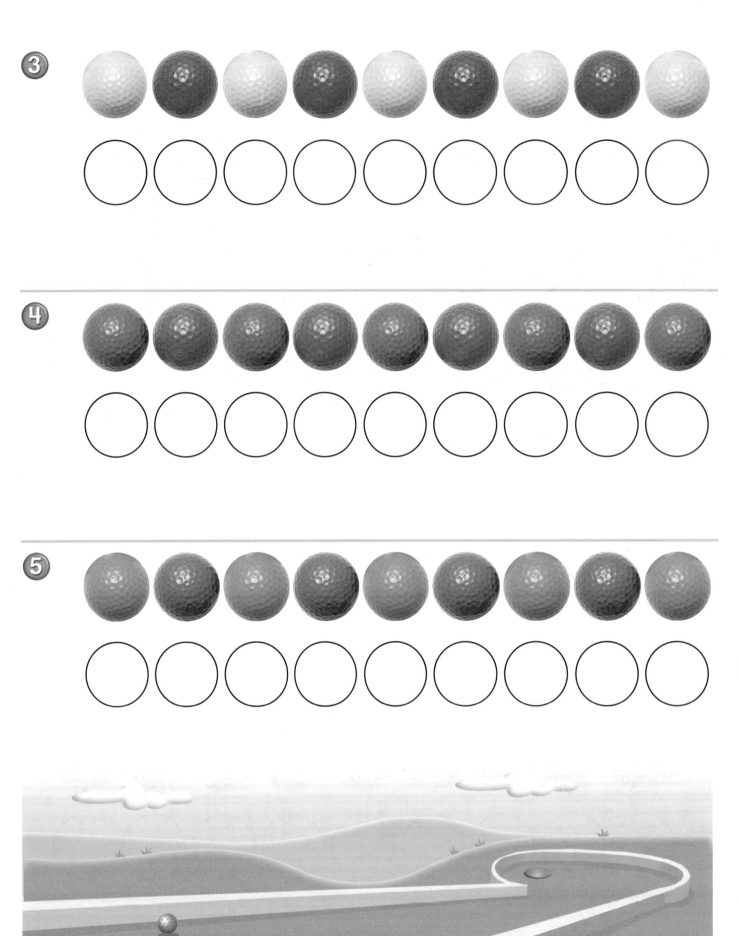

Directions 3–5: Identify each pattern. Copy the pattern by coloring the circles.

Start Smart

Name: _____

Tug of War Contest

1

2

Directions 1–2: Compare the two ropes. Circle the rope that is longer.

Directions: Compare each pair of objects. Circle the object that is longer. Place an
X on the object that is shorter.

Start Smart

Name: _____

Did you Know?

The Great Lakes Kite Festival is held in Grand Haven, Michigan.

Great Lakes Kite Festival

Directions: Trace each figure. Finish coloring the figure. Color each kite the same color as the figure it matches.

Directions: Color each circle green. Color each square blue. Color each triangle purple.
Draw another kite using a triangle, square, and circle.

Name: _____

Did you KNOW?
The bluebird is the state bird of New York.

Directions: Count how many of each color bird is in the tree. Color a space on the graph to show how many of each.

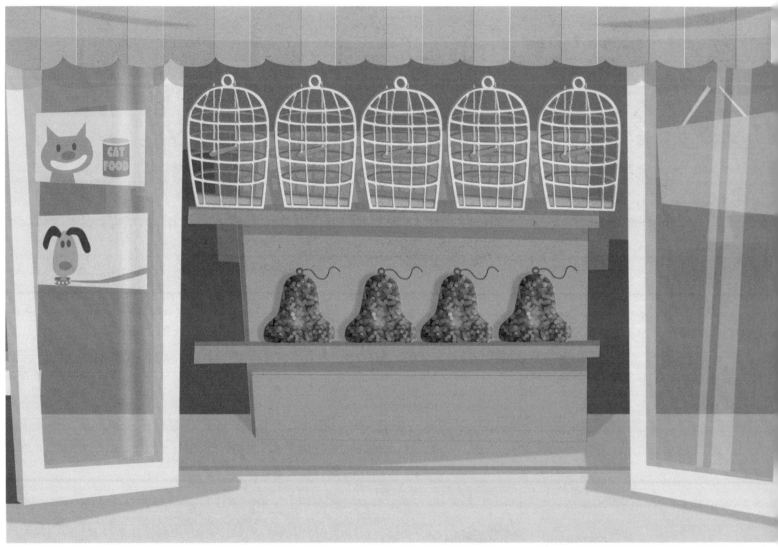

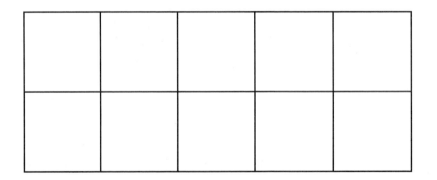

Directions: Color a space beside each object to show how many of that object there are in the store. Circle the picture that has more. Describe each object by saying how many of each object are in the store.

Start Smart

CHAPTER 1

Compare and Sort Objects

Key Vocabulary

alike

different

sort

Explore

Circle the yellow flower.

Copyright © McGraw-Hill, a division of The McGraw-Hill Companies

Name _____

✓ Are You Ready for Chapter 1?

①

②

③

④

Directions:
1. Trace the lines.
2. Circle the car. Put an X on the tree.
3. Color the truck red. Color the ball blue.
   Color the bird yellow. Color the flower purple.
4. Circle the object that is small.

This page checks skills needed for Chapter 1.

MATH at HOME

Dear Family,

Today my class started Chapter 1, **Compare and Sort Objects**. I will be learning to sort objects and to match groups of objects. Here are my vocabulary words, an activity to do, and a list of books we can read together.

Love, _____

Activity

Have your child help you sort laundry items, such as socks or food items such as canned goods.

Key Vocabulary

sort to group together items that have something in common

same number

Math Online Click on the eGlossary link at macmillanmh.com to find out more about these words. There are 13 languages.

Books to Read

Dinosaurs Are Different
by Aliki
Harper Collins Children's Books, 1986.

The Mixed-Up Chameleon
by Eric Carle
Harper Collins
Children's Books, 1984.

Is Your Mama a Llama?
by Deborah Guarino
Scholastic Press, 1997.

MATEMÁTICAS en CASA

Estimada familia,

Hoy mi clase comenzó el Capítulo I, **Compara y ordena objetos**. Aprenderé a ordenar objetos y a emparejar grupos de objetos. A continuación, están mis palabras de vocabulario, una actividad que podemos realizar y una lista de libros que podemos leer juntos.

Cariños, _____

Actividad

Pídanle a su hijo(a) que les ayude a ordenar la ropa para lavar, como las medias; o los comestibles, como los alimentos enlatados.

Vocabulario clave

ordenar agrupar objetos que tienen algo en común

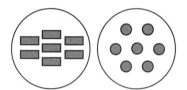

mismo número

Math Online Visiten el enlace eGlossary en macmillanmh.com para averiguar más sobre estas palabras, las cuales se muestran en 13 idiomas.

Libros para leer

Los dinosaurios son diferentes
de Aliki
Editorial Juventud, 1996.

El camaleon camaleonico
de Eric Carle
Kokinos, 2005.

¿Tu mama es una llama?
de Deborah Guarino
Scholastic Trade, 1991.

Alike and Different

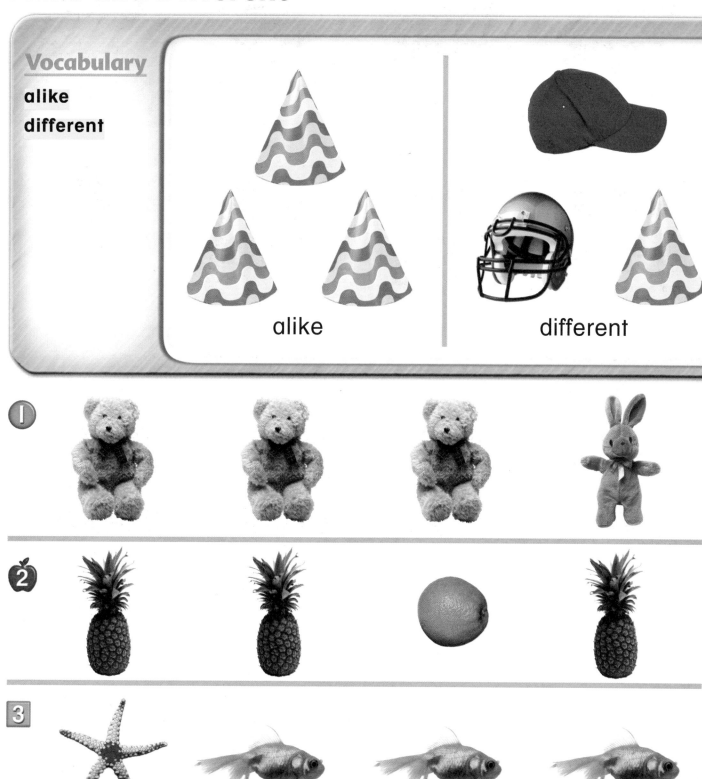

Vocabulary

alike

different

alike | different

1.

2.

3.

Directions:

1–3. Compare the objects in each row. Circle the objects that are alike. Mark an X on the one that is different. Tell how you know.

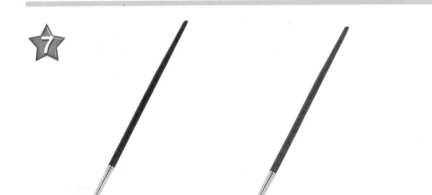

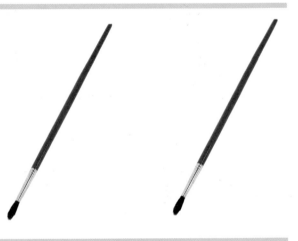

Directions:

4–7. Compare the objects in each row. Circle the objects that are alike. Mark an X on the one that is different. Tell how you know.

 Math at Home Activity: Draw a picture of some items in each room of your house. Ask your child to show which items are alike and different.

Sort by One Attribute

Copyright © Macmillan/McGraw-Hill, a division of The McGraw-Hill Companies, Inc.

Vocabulary

sort

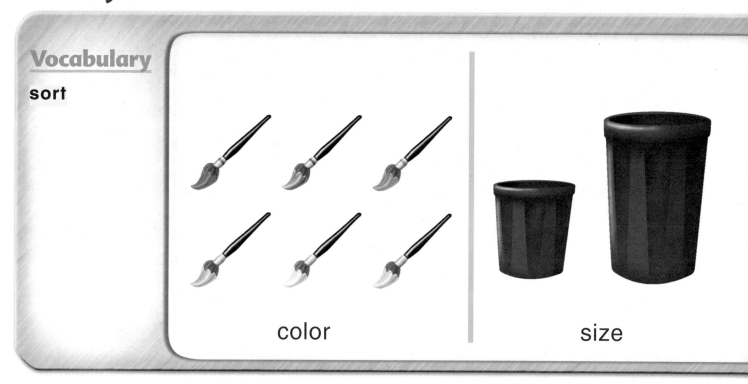

color

size

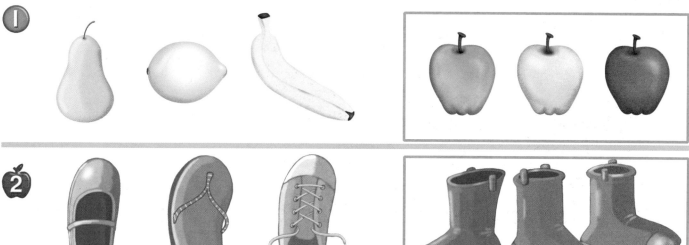

1

2

3

Directions:

1–3. Describe and identify each object in the row. Circle the object in the box that belongs in that row. Mark an X on the objects that do not belong. Tell how you know.

Chapter 1   Lesson 2

Directions: Sort the picnic items by size. Draw a line from each picnic item to the correct basket.

 Math at Home Activity: Help your child sort toys by placing all the same color toys together. Then sort another way.

Name _____

Problem-Solving Strategy
Act It Out

How can you sort the shapes?

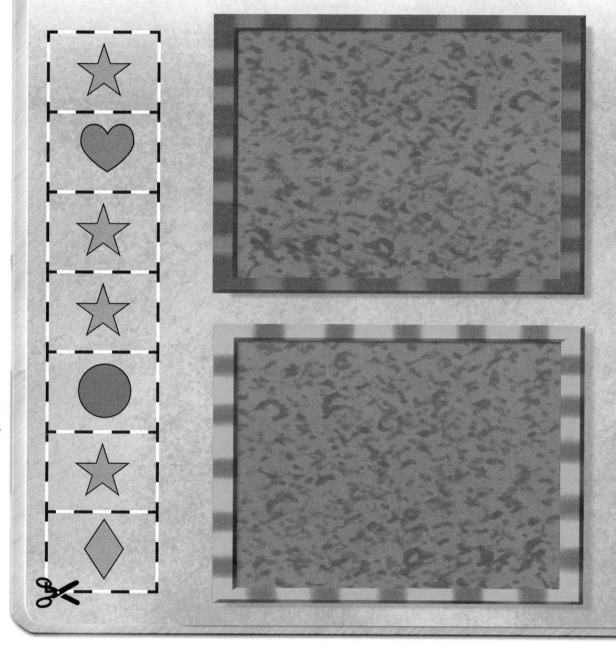

Directions: Cut out the shapes. Glue the shapes that are alike on one bulletin board. Glue the shapes that are different on the other bulletin board. Explain to a classmate how you sorted the objects.

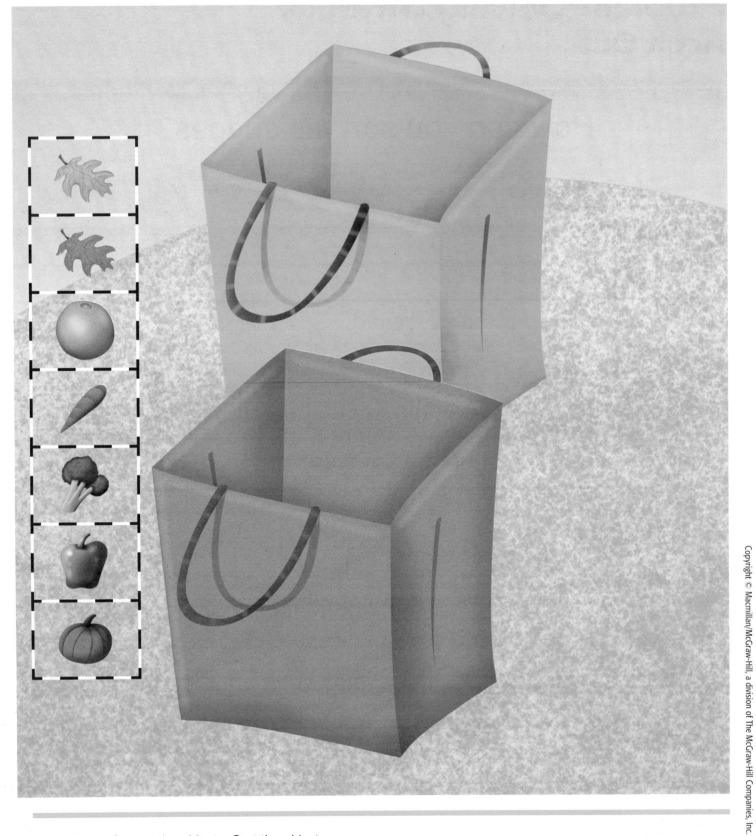

Directions: Cut out the objects. Sort the objects by color. Glue green objects in the green bag. Glue orange objects in the orange bag.

Name _____

Sort by More Than One Attribute

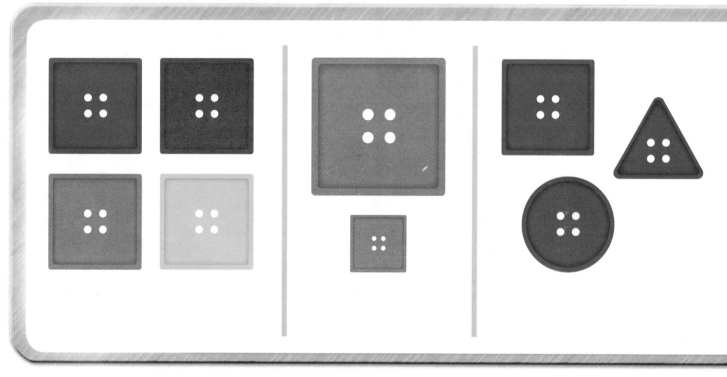

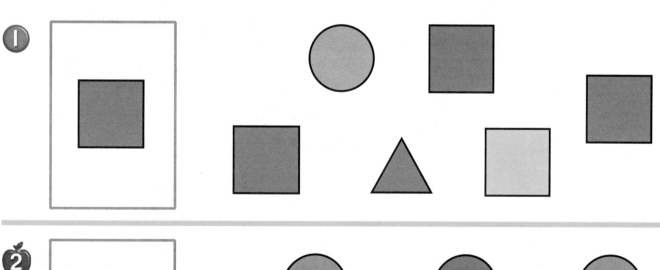

①

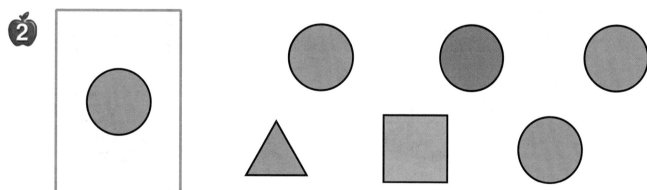

②

Directions:
1–2. Describe the colored figure in the box. Circle the figures in the group that are like the figure in the box. Put an X on the figures that are different from the figure in the box. Tell how you know.

Chapter 1   Lesson 4   twenty-three   **23**

Directions:

3–6. Describe the size and color of the object in the box. Circle the objects that are like the object in the box. Put an X on the objects that are different from the object in the box. Tell how you know.

Math at Home Activity: Using shoes from all family members, ask your child to sort the shoes into groups such as small white shoes or large brown shoes.

Chapter 1   Lesson 4

Name _____

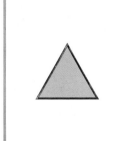

Directions:
1–2. Circle the objects that are alike. Mark an X on the object that is different.
3. Sort the color tiles by drawing a line from each color tile to the same color bag.
4. Describe the colored figure in the box. Circle the figures in the group that are like the object in the box.
   Put an X on the figures that are different from the object in the box.

Button Up!
Sorting

You Will Need

Play with a partner. Take turns.
- Put your ⬛ on **Start**.
- Spin the 🕐.
- Move your cube to the next star of that color.
- Take any figure or size attribute button that is this same color.
- First player to reach **Finish** wins!

Name _____

Same Number

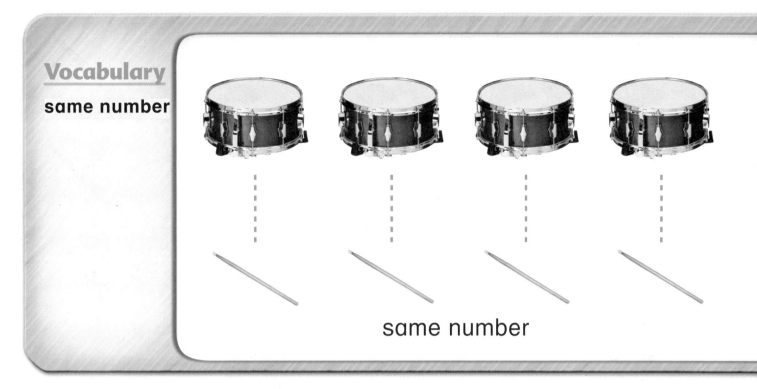

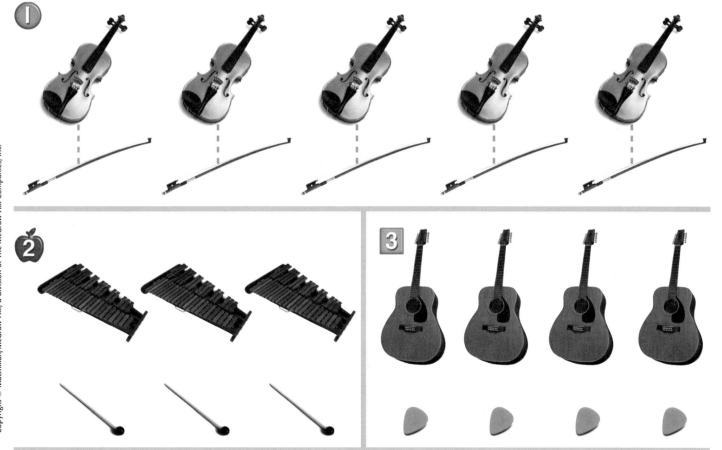

Directions:
1. Trace lines to match the objects in the two groups. Describe the sizes of the two groups of objects.
2–3. Draw lines to match the objects in the two groups. Describe the sizes of the two groups of objects.

Chapter 1   Lesson 5   twenty-seven   **27**

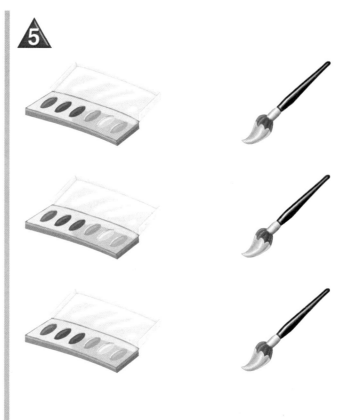

Directions:
4–5. Draw lines to match the objects in the two groups.
6–7. Use color tiles to create a group that is the same number as the group of objects shown. Trace the color tiles. Draw lines to show that the groups have the same number.

 Math at Home Activity: Gather four spoons, three pencils, and five pennies. Ask your child to gather the same number of objects. Match them to show the same number.

Name _____

More Than

Vocabulary

more than

more than

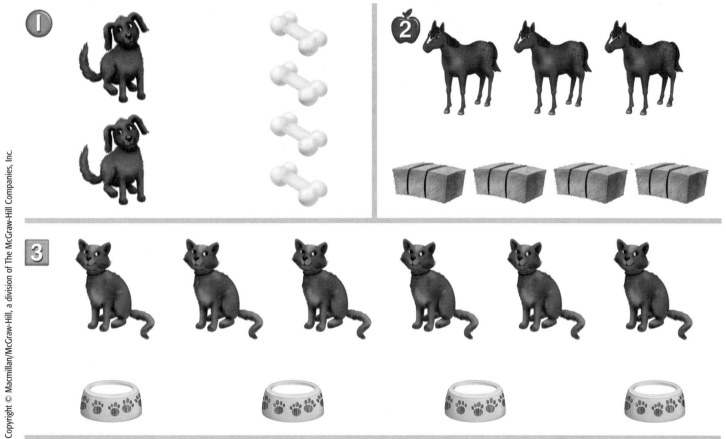

Directions:

1–3. Draw lines to match objects in the two groups.
Describe the sizes of the two groups of objects.
Circle the group that has more than the other group.

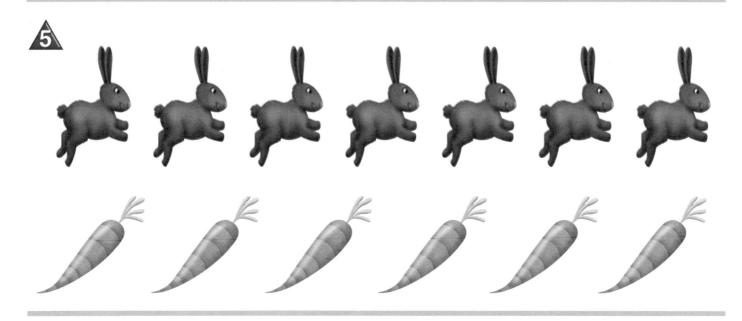

Directions:

4–5. Draw lines to match objects in the two groups. Circle the group that has more than the other group.

6. Use color tiles to show a group with more tiles than pigs. Trace the tiles.

Math at Home Activity: Show 7 fingers. Have your child show more fingers; the same number of fingers.

Chapter 1   Lesson 6

Name _____

Less Than

Copyright © Macmillan/McGraw-Hill, a division of The McGraw-Hill Companies, Inc.

Vocabulary

less than

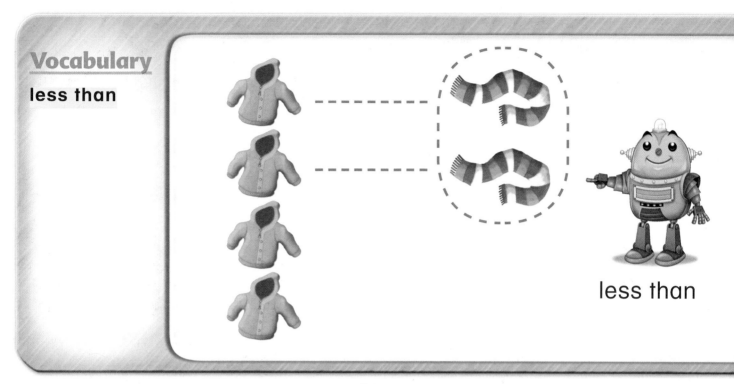

less than

Directions:

1–3. Draw a line from an object in one group to match an object in the other group. Circle the group that has less. Describe the sizes of the two sets of objects.

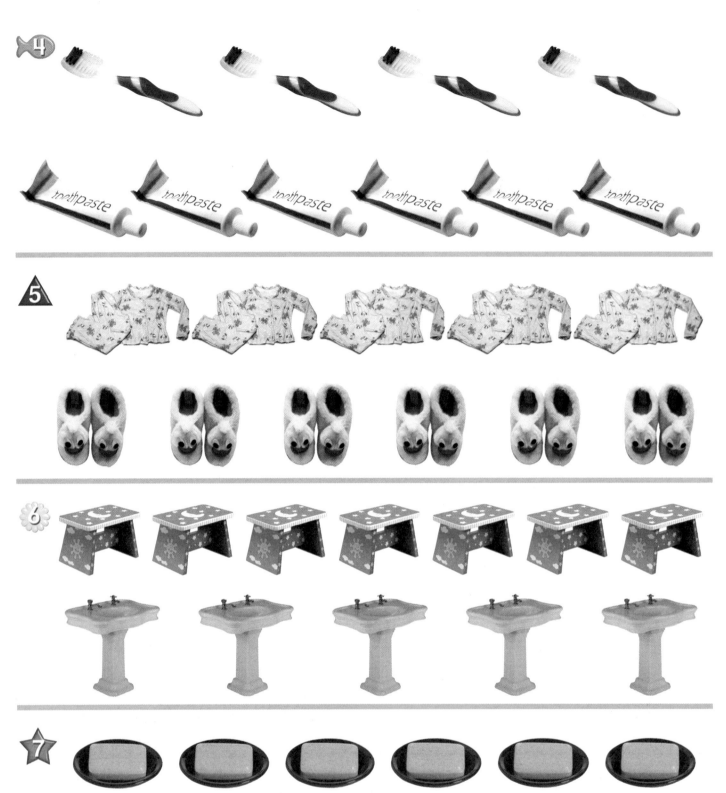

Directions:

4–6. Draw a line from an object in one group to match an object in the other group. Circle the group that has less objects.

7. Use color tiles to show a group with less tiles than bars of soap. Trace the tiles.

Math at Home Activity: Gather three pencils and five crayons. Compare pencils and crayons. Discuss less than.

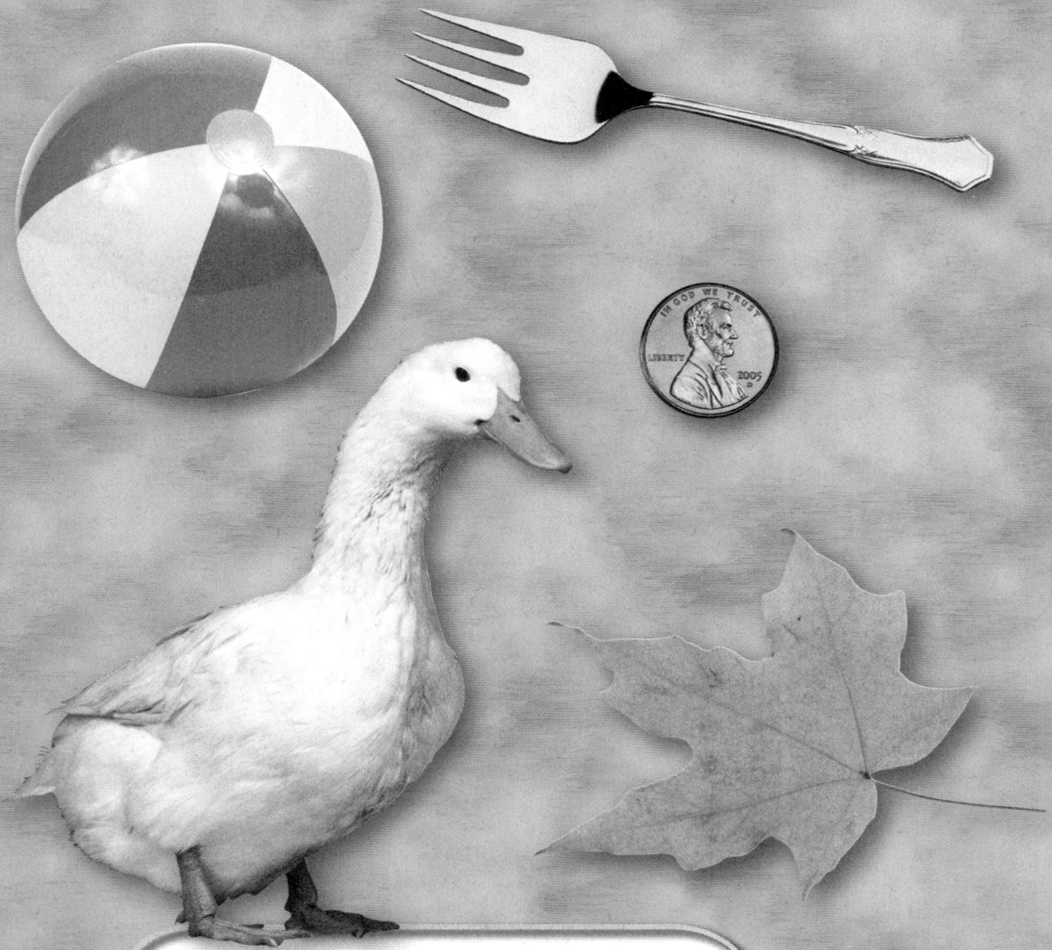

Circle the items that float. Put an X on the items that sink. Are there more that float or sink? Circle your answer.

Float   Sink

FOLD DOWN

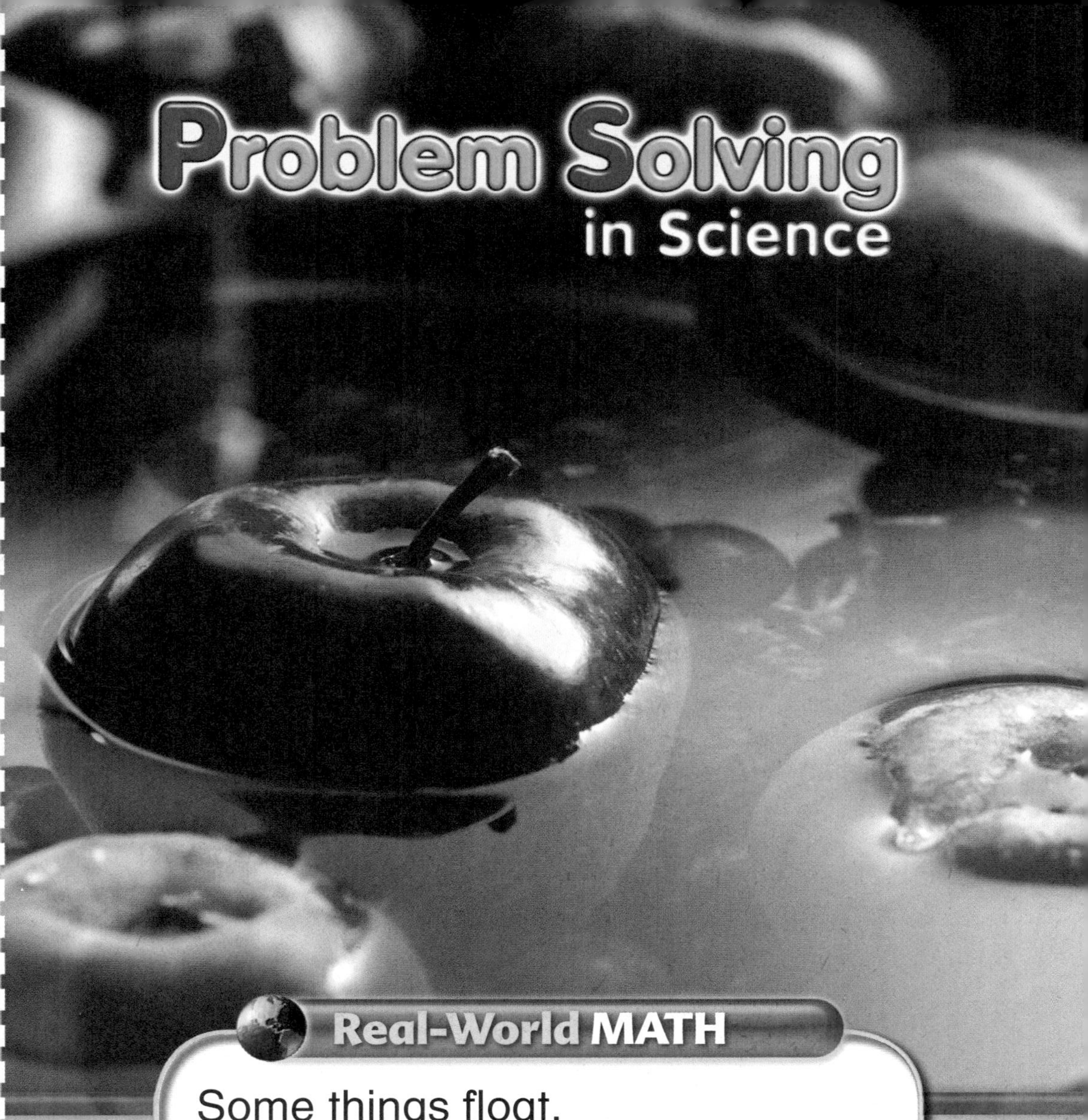

Problem Solving in Science

Real-World MATH

Some things float.
Some things sink.

This book belongs to

_____

Silverware sinks.

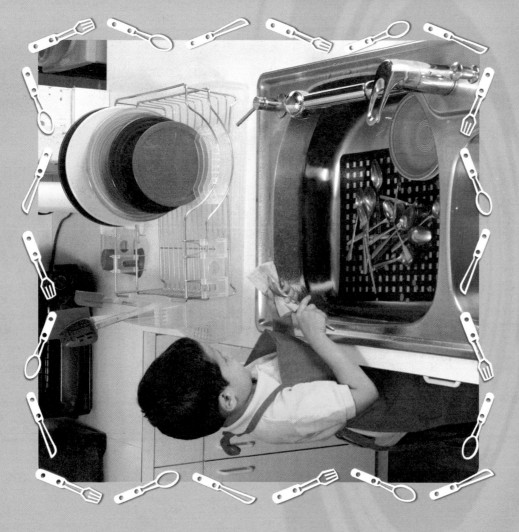

Some toys float.

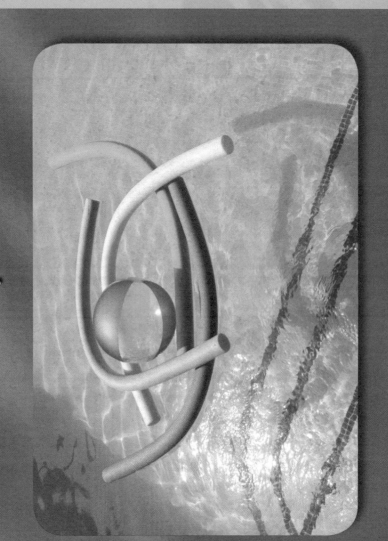

Name _____

1

2

3

Directions:
1. Sort the cans by color. Draw a line from each soup can to where it belongs.
2. Draw a line from each object in one group to match an object in the other group.
3. Draw a line from each object in one group to match an object in the other group. Circle the group that has less objects than the other group.

Chapter 1   thirty-five   **35**

Name

Directions:

1. Circle the objects that are alike. Mark an X on the object that is different.
2. Look at the pillow in the box. Circle the pillows that are like the pillow in the box. Mark an X on the pillows that are different from the one in the box.
3. Draw a line from each object in one group to match an object in the other group. Circle the group that shows more objects than the other group.

Name _____

1.

$\bigcirc$ $\bigcirc$ $\bigcirc$

2.

$\bigcirc$ $\bigcirc$ $\bigcirc$

3.

$\bigcirc$ $\bigcirc$ $\bigcirc$

4.

$\bigcirc$ $\bigcirc$ $\bigcirc$

Directions: Listen as the teacher reads each problem. Choose the correct answer.

5.

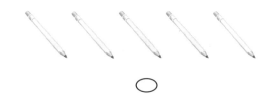

◯　　　　　　　　◯　　　　　　　　◯

6.

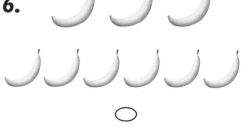

◯　　　　　　　◯　　　　　　　◯

7.

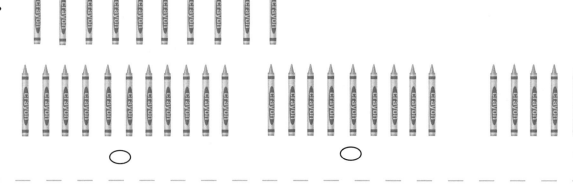

◯　　　　　　　◯　　　　　　　◯

8.

◯　　　　　　　◯　　　　　　　◯

Directions: Listen as the teacher reads each problem. Choose the correct answer.

Summative Assessment

CHAPTER 2

Use Numbers 0 to 5

Key Vocabulary

count
number
order

Explore

How many raccoons?
How many noses?

Chapter 2

thirty-nine **39**

Math Online

Take the Chapter Readiness
Quiz at macmillanmh.com.

Are You Ready for Chapter 2?

1

2

3

4

Directions:

1. Match each cat to one cat bed by drawing a line.
2. Color 3 apples.
3. Look at the picture. Count the flower(s). Draw that many flower(s).
4. Look at the picture. Count the baseballs. Draw that many baseballs.

This page checks skills needed for Chapter 2.

MATH at HOME

Dear Family,

Today my class started Chapter 2, **Use Numbers 0 to 5.** I will learn to count and compare numbers zero to five. Here are my vocabulary words, an activity we can do, and a list of books we can read together.

Love, _____

Activity

Ask your child to count different objects. For example, ask how many pillows are on the bed, how many plates are on the table, or how many cans are in the cupboard.

Key Vocabulary

count

1   2   3

order 1, 3, 6, 7, 9

these numbers are in order from smallest to largest

Math Online ▷ Click on the eGlossary link at macmillanmh.com to find out more about these words. There are 13 languages.

Books to Read

1 2 3
How Many Animals Can You See?
by Emilie Boon
Orchard Books,
1996.

1, 2, 3 To the Zoo
by Eric Carle
Putnam, 1998.

At the Edge of the Woods:
A Counting Book
by Cynthia Cotten
Henry Holt and Co.,
2002.

Estimada Familia,

Hoy mi clase comenzó el Capítulo 2, **Usa los números desde el 0 hasta el 5**. Aprenderé a contar y a comparar los números del cero al cinco. A continuación, están mis palabras de vocabulario, una actividad que podemos realizar y una lista de libros que podemos leer juntos.

Cariños,

_____

Actividad

Pídanle a su hijo(a) que cuente diferentes objetos. Por ejemplo, pregúntenle cuántas almohadas hay en la cama, cuántos platos hay en la mesa o cuántas latas hay en la alacena.

Vocabulario clave

contar   ⚫ ⚫ ⚪
        1   2   3

ordenar   1, 3, 6, 7, 9
estos números están en order del menor al mayor

Math Online ▷ Visiten el enlace eGlossary en macmillanmh.com para averiguar más sobre estas palabras, las cuales se muestran en 13 idiomas.

Libros recomendados

Los cinco patitos
de Pam Paparone
North South Books, 2007.

1, 2, 3, Gatitos
de Michael Van Zeveren
Ekaré Express, 2006.

Numbers 1, 2, and 3

Vocabulary

count

one

two

three

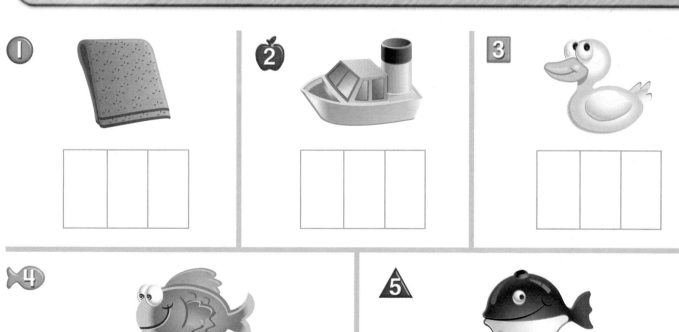

Directions:

1–5. Identify the object. Use the picture above to count how many of that object. Use color tiles to show that many of each object. Color one box for each object counted. Say that number.

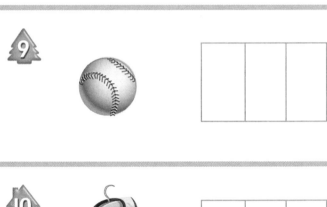

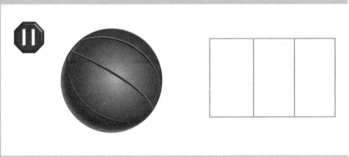

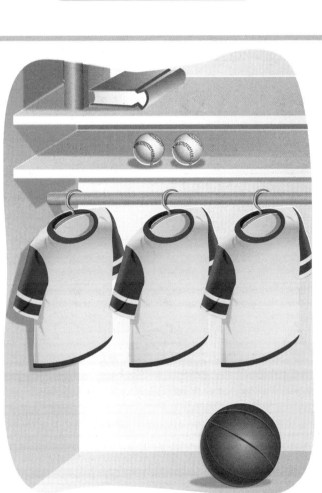

Directions:

6–11. Identify the object. Use the picture to count how many of that object. Use color tiles to show that many of each object. Color one box for each object counted. Say that number.

 Math at Home Activity: Gather items such as paper clips, rubber bands, or sheets of paper. Put them in groups of one, two, and three. Practice counting the items in each group.

44 forty-four

Chapter 2 Lesson 1

Name _____

Read and Write 1, 2, and 3

Vocabulary

number

I
one

3
three

2
two

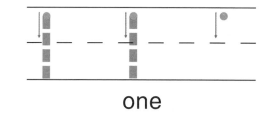

one

two

three

Copyright © Macmillan/McGraw-Hill, a division of The McGraw-Hill Companies, Inc.

Directions:
1. Draw one butterfly. Trace the number 1. Write the number 1.
2. Draw two baseballs. Trace the number 2. Write the number 2.
3. Draw three flowers. Trace the number 3. Write the number 3.

Chapter 2   Lesson 2

forty-five   **45**

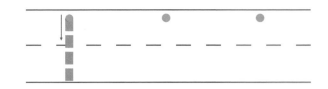

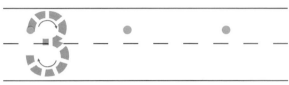

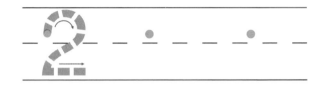

Directions:

4–6. Count the objects in each row. Say the number. Trace and write the number.

 Math at Home Activity: Show your child 3 spoons, 2 cups, and 1 bowl. Count how many of each. Write that number.

7–8. Count the objects in each row. Say the number. Write that number three times.

Chapter 2 Lesson 2

Name

Numbers 4 and 5

Vocabulary
four
five

4
four

5
five

(1)

(2)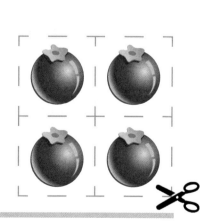

Directions:
1. Draw 5 berries on the bush.
2. Cut out the berries and glue 4 berries on the bush.

Chapter 2   Lesson 3

forty-seven   **47**

Directions: Count each group of bees. Say the number. Circle each group of four bees. Place an X on each group of five bees.

Math at Home Activity: Help your child gather objects such as pennies, cups, or toy figures. Put objects in groups of four and groups of five. Practice counting the objects in each group.

Name

Read and Write 4 and 5

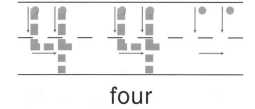

four

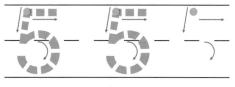

five

Directions:
1. Draw four cones. Trace the number 4. Write the number 4.
2. Draw five bricks. Trace the number 5. Write the number 5.

3

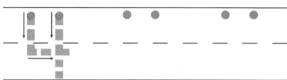

4

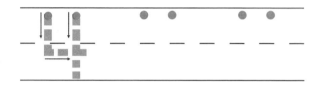

5

6

7

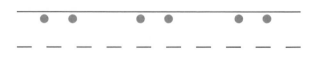

Directions:

3–5. Count the objects in each row. Say the number. Trace and write the number.

6–7. Count the objects in each row. Write that number three times.

 Math at Home Activity: Make groups of 4 and 5 using cereal or macaroni. Have your child count how many in each group and write that number.

Chapter 2 Lesson 4

Name _____

_____
_ _ _ _
_____

_____
_ _ _ _
_____

Directions:
1. Count each object. Color a box for each object counted. Write the number.
2. Circle each group of five frogs. Place an X on each group of four frogs.
3. Count the objects. Write the number.

Chapter 2

Rainbow Crossing

Counting

Copyright © Macmillan/McGraw-Hill, a division of The McGraw-Hill Companies, Inc.

You Will Need

10

Play with a partner. Take turns.

○ Roll the .

○ Move your cube that number of spaces.

○ If you land on:

Red–take 1

Blue–put 1 back

Yellow–wait until next turn

○ When both players reach **Finish**, count to see who has more .

Problem-Solving Strategy
Draw a Picture

How many ducks?

Draw

Directions: Draw a line from the ring at the end of each fishing line to a duck. Draw a circle for each duck that was caught. Explain your drawing. Tell how many ducks were caught.

Chapter 2   Lesson 5

Directions: Each child caught one duck. Draw a line from each child's pole to the duck that was caught. Draw one circle for each duck that was not caught. Tell how many ducks were not caught.

Math at Home Activity: Take advantage of problem-solving opportunities during daily routines such as going to the grocery store. Have your child help you make the grocery list by drawing pictures of the grocery items needed.

Read and Write 0

Copyright © Macmillan/McGraw-Hill, a division of The McGraw-Hill Companies, Inc.

Vocabulary

zero

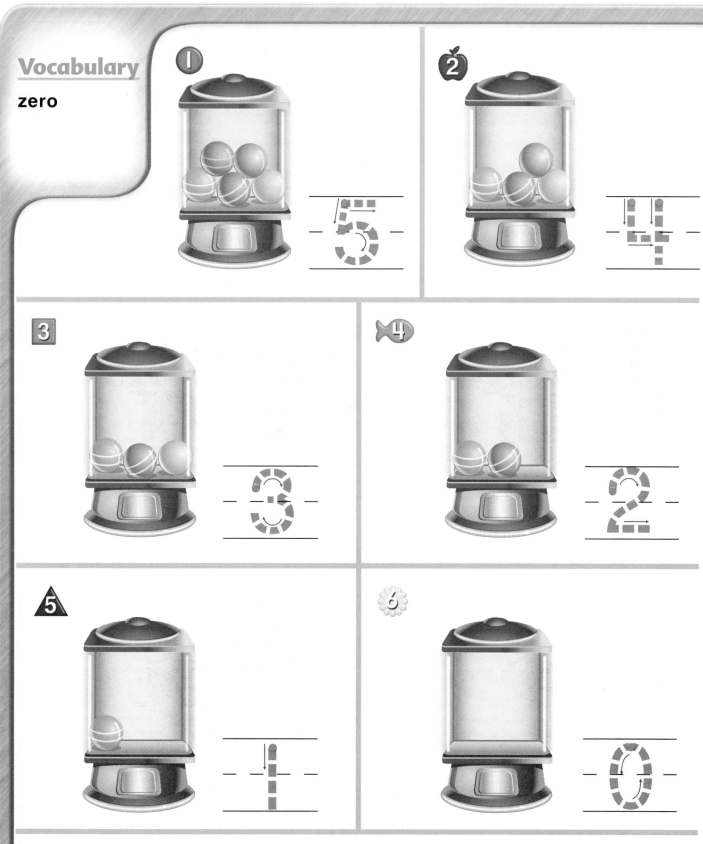

Directions:

1–6. Count how many balls in each machine. Say the number. Write the number that shows how many.

_____
- - - - - -
_____

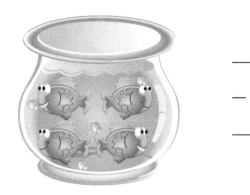

_____
- - - - - -
_____

_____
- - - - - -
_____

_____
- - - - - -
_____

_____
- - - - - -
_____

_____
- - - - - -
_____

Directions:
7–8. Write how many fish are in the fish bowl.
9–10. Write how many cats are in the box.
11–12. Write how many puppies are in the wagon.

Math at Home Activity: Look at a family photo. Ask your child questions that will give zero as the answer. Practice writing the number zero with your child.

Chapter 2   Lesson 6

Name _____

Compare Numbers 0 to 5

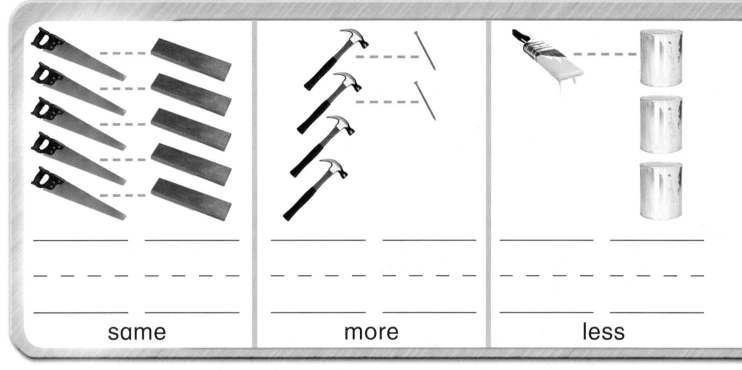

| same | more | less |

1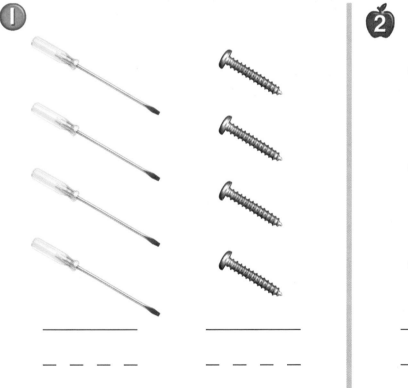

2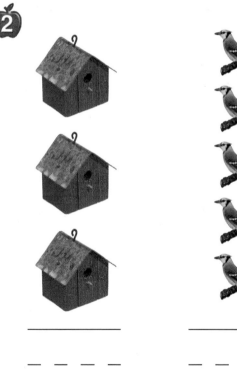

Directions:

1–2. Draw lines to match the objects in one set with the other. Say and write the number in each set. Put an X on the set and number that has more. Put a circle around the set and number that has less. Draw a box around the sets and numbers that are the same.

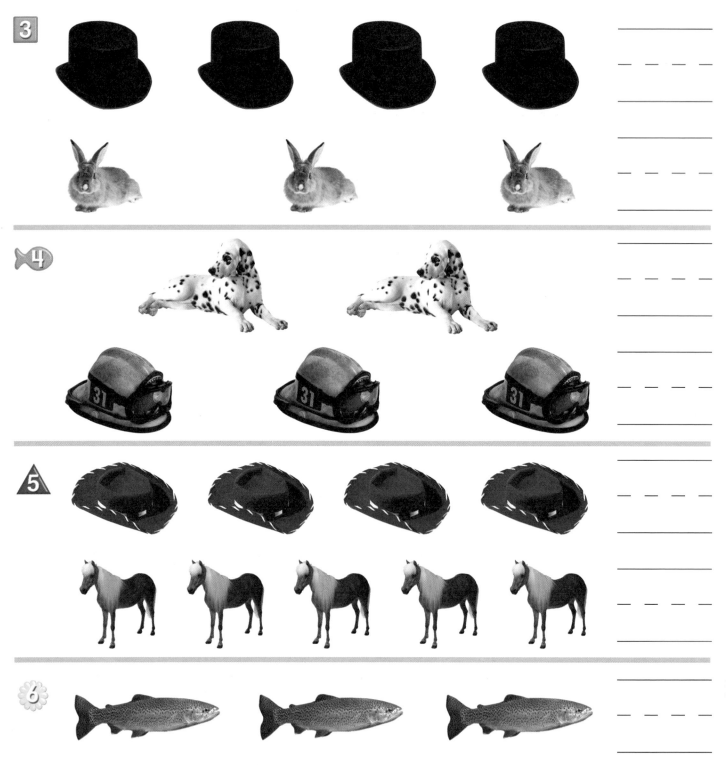

Directions:

3–4. Draw lines to match the objects in each row. Write the number. Put an X on the set and number that has more.

5. Draw a line to match the objects in each row. Write the number. Circle the set and number that has less.

6. Draw a set that has less. Write the number in each set.

Math at Home Activity: Make two groups of toys or books, up to 5 items, in each group. Ask your child which group has more, which has less, or which groups have the same number. Write the numbers. Practice with other groupings.

Name _____

Order Numbers 0 to 5

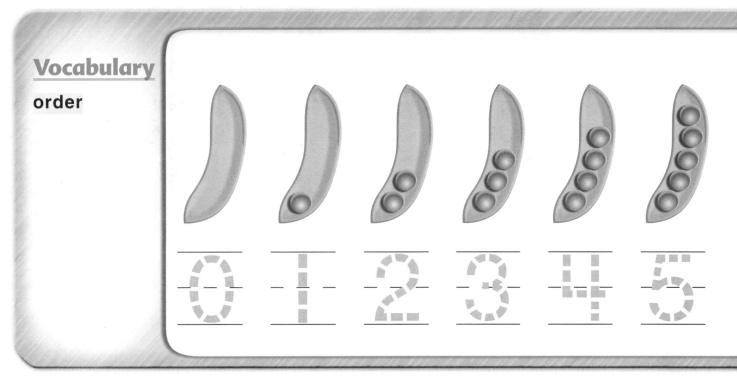

1

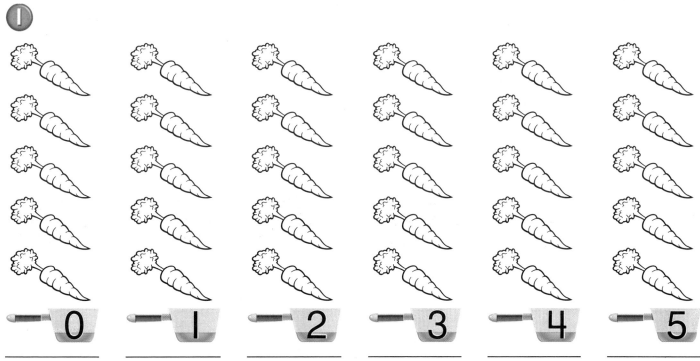

Directions:
1. Identify the number. Say the number. Color that number of carrots.
   Write the numbers in order from 0 to 5.

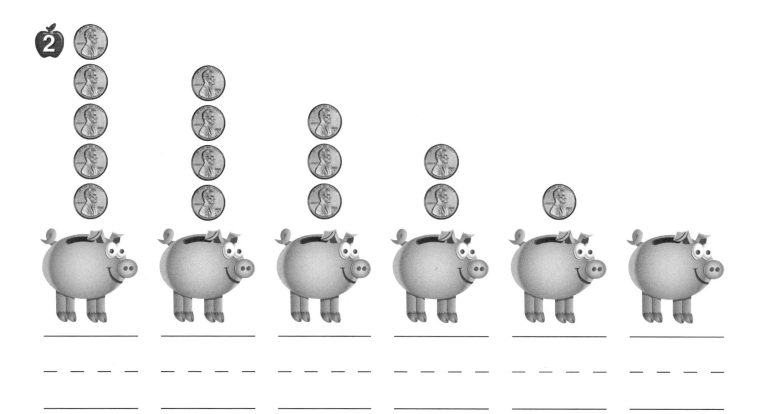

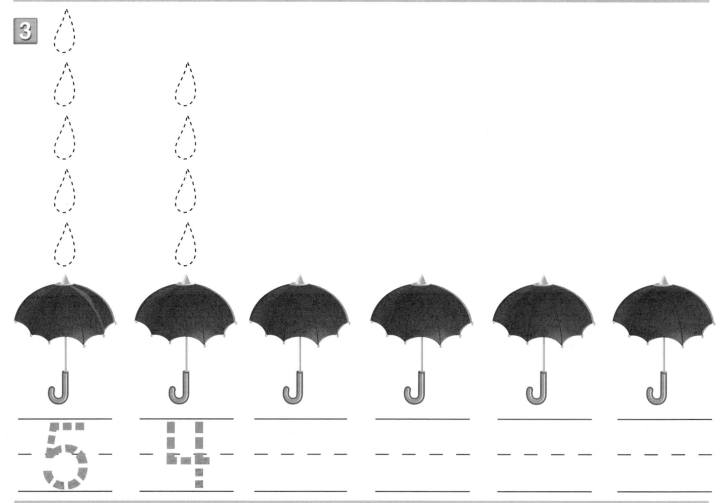

Directions:

2. Count the pennies going into each bank. Write the number on the line.
3. Identify the number. Trace it. Draw that many raindrops. Write the remaining numbers in order and draw the raindrops to show how many.

 Math at Home Activity: Write numbers 0 through 5 on paper. Use one paper per number. Find objects to place on the sheets of paper to show that number. Talk about order of numbers.

60 sixty   Chapter 2   Lesson 8

D

Here are more shoppers!

How many people do you see?

_____ people

FOLD DOWN

A

Problem Solving
in Social Studies

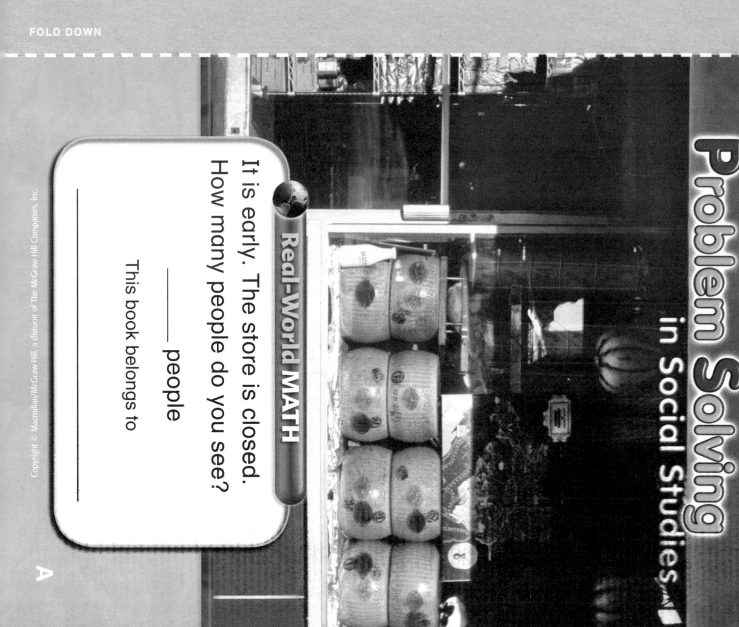

Real-World MATH

It is early. The store is closed.
How many people do you see?

_____ people

This book belongs to

_____

Here is the baker.

How many people want to buy bread?

—— people

Here is a store worker.

How many people do you see?

—— person

C

B

Name _____

1

_ _ _ _ _ _

2

3

| 0 | 1 | 2 | 3 | 4 | 5 |

____ ____ ____ ____ ____ ____

Directions:
1. Write how many fish are in the fish bowl.
2. Draw a line from each object in one row to an object in the row below.
   Count the objects in each row. Write the number. Put an X on the
   group and number that is more.
3. Identify the number. Color the number of basketballs shown on the hoop.
   Write the numbers in order from 0 to 5.

Chapter 2

Name _____

1

2

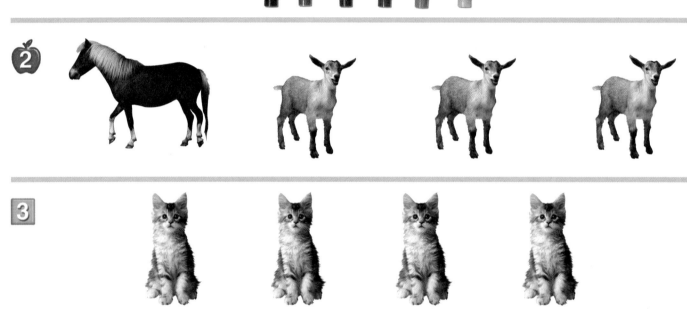

3

4

Directions:
1. Draw a line from each object in one group to match an object in the other group. Circle the group that has less.
2. Circle the objects that are the same. Mark an X on the objects that are different.
3. Draw a line from each object in one group to match an object in the other group.
4. Count the objects. Write the number.

Name _____

1.

3

     ⬭   ⬭   ⬭

2.

    1   3   4
    ⬭   ⬭   ⬭

3.

                        ⬭   ⬭   ⬭

4.

    ⬭   ⬭   ⬭

Directions: Listen as your teacher reads each problem. Choose the correct answer.

Chapter 2

sixty-five **65**

5.

◯   ◯   ◯

6.

◯   ◯   ◯

7.

0   1   2

◯   ◯   ◯

8.

1   2   3

◯   ◯   ◯

Directions: Listen as your teacher reads each problem. Choose the correct answer.

Summative Assessment

Describe Position and Patterns

Key Vocabulary

top
middle
bottom
pattern

Explore

What colors are the stripes on the zebra's face?

Name _____

Math Online ▶
Take the Chapter Readiness
Quiz at macmillanmh.com.

✓ Are You Ready for Chapter 3?

①

②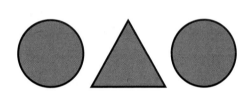

3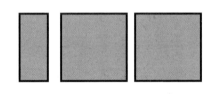

④

Directions:
1. Color the first paintbrush yellow, the second blue, the third red, and the fourth green. Draw a line to match each brush to the same color paint.
2–3. Circle the figure that is different.
4. Copy the figures by drawing them in the space below.

This page checks skills needed for Chapter 3.

MATH at HOME

Dear Family,

Today my class started Chapter 3, **Describe Position and Patterns**. I will be learning about position words and how to find and create patterns using objects, sounds, and movements. Here are my vocabulary words, an activity we can do, and a list of books we can read together.

Love, _____

Activity

Make up clap, slap, stomp patterns and have your child copy them. Repeat each pattern 3 times. When your child can repeat your patterns, switch.

Key Vocabulary

top →
middle →
bottom →

pattern

pattern unit →

Math Online Click on the eGlossary link at macmillanmh.com to find out more about this word. There are 13 languages.

Books to Read

Five Little Monkeys Jumping on the Bed
by Eileen Christelow
Clarion Books, 1998.

Jump, Frog, Jump!
by Robert Kalan
Harper Collins
Publishers, 1989.

Pattern Fish
by Trudy Harris
Lerner Publishing
Group, 2000.

Estimada familia:

Hoy mi clase comenzó el Capítulo 3, **Describe posiciones y patrones**. Aprenderé acerca de palabras que tengan que ver con posición y a encontrar y hacer patrones con colores tamaños y formas. A continuación, están mis palabras de vocabulario, una actividad que podemos realizar y una lista de libros que podemos leer juntos.

Cariños,

_____

Actividad

Inventen patrones de aplausos, palmadas y pisadas fuertes y pídanle a su hijo(a) que los repita. Repitan 3 veces cada patrón. Cuando su hijo(a) repita fácilmente sus patrones, cámbienlos.

Vocabulario clave

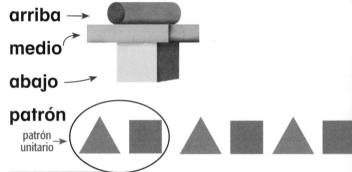

arriba →
medio →
abajo →

patrón

patrón unitario

Math Online > Visiten el enlace eGlossary en macmillanmh.com para averiguar más sobre estas palabras, las cuales se muestran en 13 idiomas.

Libros recomendados

Cinco monitos brincando en la cama
de Eileen Christelow
Clarion Books, 2005.

¡Salta, Ranita, Salta!
de Robert Kalan
Live Oak Media, 2005

¿Patrones: Que hay en la pared?
de John Burstein
Gareth Stevens
Publishing, 2006

Over and Under

Vocabulary

over

above

under

below

Directions:

1. Describe the position of each banana using the words over, under, above, or below. Circle the bananas that are over or above a monkey. Underline bananas that are under or below a monkey.
2. Place a yellow color tile under or below each monkey. Draw a banana where you placed each color tile.

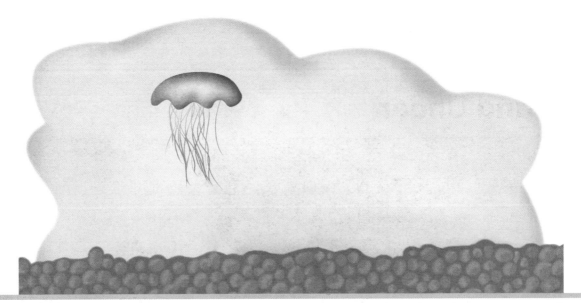

Directions:

3–4. Place a blue color tile above the object. Place a yellow color tile below the object. Draw a fish where you placed each color tile.

5. Describe the position of each fish using the words over, under, above, or below. Circle the fish that is above or over. Put an X on the fish that is under or below.

Math at Home Activity: When cleaning at home, give your child directions using the words above, below, over, and under. For example: Put your shoes on the floor below the coats in the closet. Stack these books above the games on the shelf.

Name _____

Top, Middle, and Bottom

Vocabulary

top

middle

bottom

Directions: Place a red color tile on the bottom blanket. Place a yellow color tile on the middle blanket. Place a green tile on the top blanket. Color the blankets to match the color tiles.

Directions:

1–2. Put an X on the object on top.
3. Circle the object on the bottom.
4. Circle the flower on the bottom.
5–6. Put an X on the object in the middle.

 Math at Home Activity: Play "I Spy" with your child. Have him or her find things that are on top, in the middle, or on the bottom of something else. Use those words in your description of the object.

74 seventy-four

Chapter 3   Lesson 2

Name _____

Before and After

Vocabulary

before
after

1

2

Directions:
1. Place a color tile on the rooster that is before the chick. Circle the rooster.
2. Is the yellow duck before or after the frog? Circle the animal that is before the frog.

3

4

5

6

Directions:

3–4. Place a yellow color tile on the animal that is before the other animals. Circle it. Place a blue color tile on the animal that is after the other animals. Put an X on that animal.

5. Is the blue bird before or after the red bird? Circle the bird that is before the blue bird.

6. Is the brown horse before or after the white horse? Circle the horse that is after the black horse.

Math at Home Activity: Have your child help you make dinner. Ask him or her what you will need to do before you start cooking or what you will need to do after you are done eating. After you eat, ask your child questions about what you did together using the words before and after.

Name _____

Identify Patterns

Vocabulary

pattern

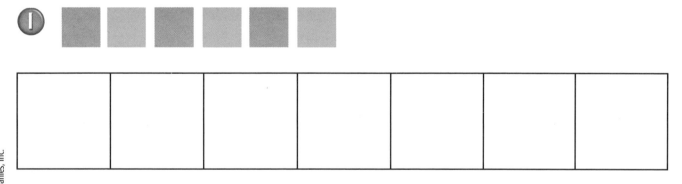

**① **

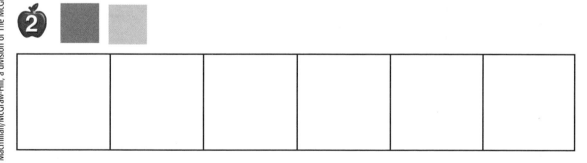

**② **

Directions:

1. Identify the pattern. Use color tiles to copy and extend the pattern. Color the boxes to show the pattern.

2. Use color tiles to create your own pattern using the two tile colors shown. Color the boxes to show the pattern you created. Explain your pattern.

Chapter 3   Lesson 4

seventy-seven   **77**

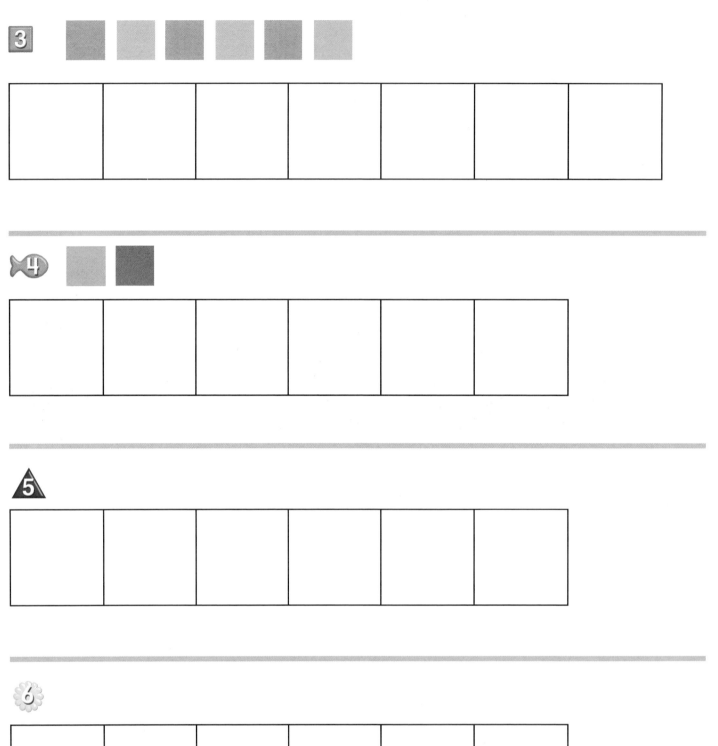

Directions:

3. Identify the pattern. Use color tiles to create and extend the pattern. Color the boxes to show the pattern.

4. Create your own pattern using the two tile colors shown. Color the boxes to show your pattern.

5–6. Use two colors to create your own pattern using color tiles. Color the boxes to show the pattern you created. Explain your pattern.

 Math at Home Activity: Have your child find something in your home that represents an AB pattern.

Name

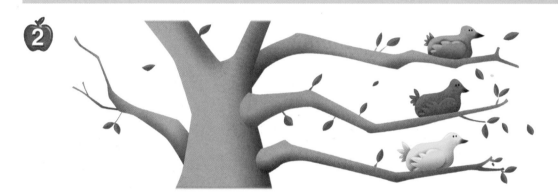

Directions:
1. Circle the balloon that is above the tree.
2. Underline the bird on the middle branch. Put an X on the bird on the top branch.
3. Circle the car that is before the red truck. Put an X on the car that is after the gray car.
4. Underline the object that could come next in the pattern.

Chapter 3

seventy-nine 79

Pattern Strings
Patterning

You Will Need

2

Play with a partner. Take turns.

- Take a string. Copy your pattern.
- Roll .
- Move your cube that many spaces.
- If you land on the color that comes next in your pattern, add the correct button to your string. If not, wait for your next turn.
- The first person to put 4 more buttons on their string is the winner.

Start →

80   eighty

Name _____

Object Patterns

1

2

Copyright © Macmillan/McGraw-Hill, a division of The McGraw-Hill Companies, Inc.

Directions:
1–2. Identify the pattern. Use attribute buttons to create the pattern.
Circle the button that could come next in the pattern. Explain.

Chapter 3   Lesson 5

eighty-one   81

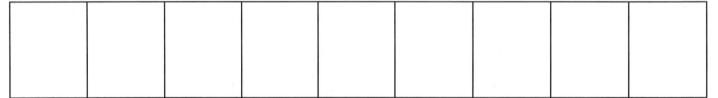

Directions:

3–5. Use attribute buttons to create the pattern. Circle the button that could come next in the pattern. Explain.

6. Use the buttons shown to create your own pattern. Color the boxes to show your pattern another way.

 Math at Home Activity: Have your child use canned goods and boxes of food to create his or her own pattern. Ask him or her to explain the pattern by telling you why they put the objects in a certain order.

Name _____

Problem-Solving Strategy
Look for a Pattern

Can you show this another way?

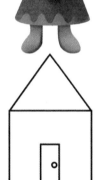

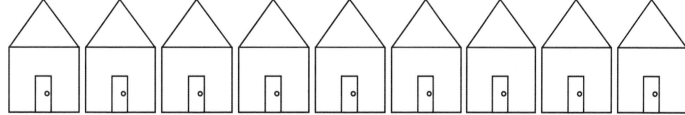

Directions:

1. Look at the row. Identify the pattern. Create a different pattern using color tiles. Color the houses to show the pattern. Explain your pattern.

2

3

Directions:

2. Look at the row. Identify the pattern. Create a different pattern using color tiles. Color the stars to show the pattern. Explain your pattern.
3. Look at the pictures in the row. Identify the pattern. Draw shapes to create a pattern to match. Explain your pattern.

 Math at Home Activity: Take advantage of problem-solving opportunities during daily routines such as riding in the car, bedtime, doing laundry, putting away groceries, planning schedules, and so on.

Name _____

Sound Patterns

1

2

3

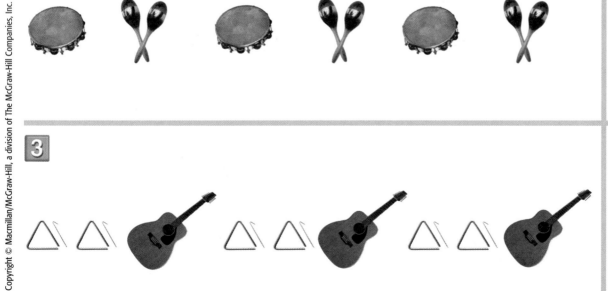   

Directions:

1–3. Identify the pattern. Extend the pattern by circling the instrument that makes the sound that could come next.

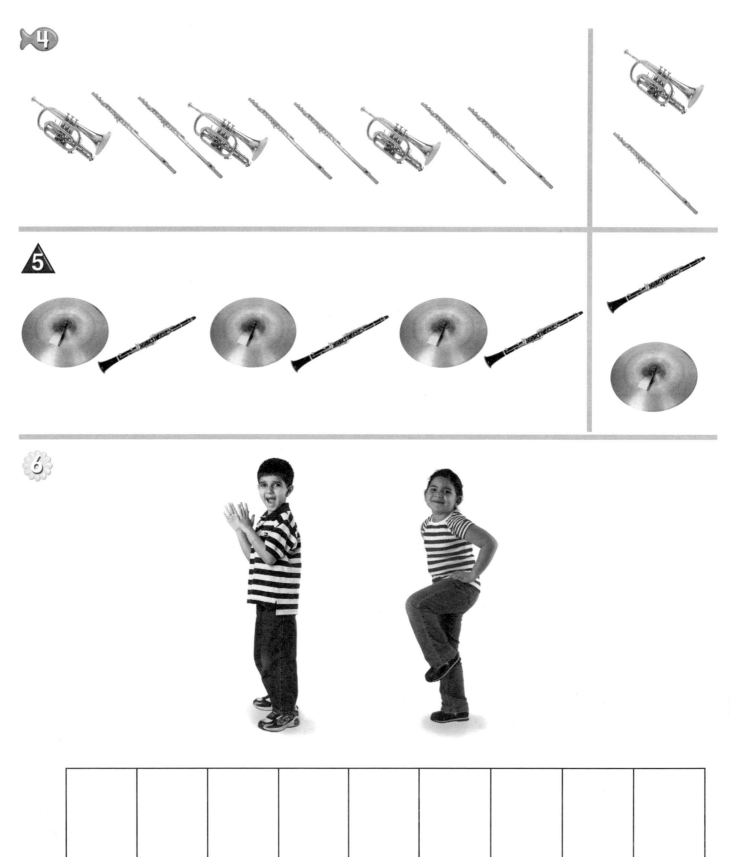

Directions:

4–5. Extend the pattern by circling the instrument that makes the sound that could come next.

6. Create a sound pattern using the sounds shown. Show your pattern another way in the boxes.

 Math at Home Activity: Have your child create different sound patterns using a wooden or plastic spoon, different size pots, and plastic containers. Have him or her create an AB, ABB, and AAB pattern by hitting the pots and containers with the spoon.

Name _____

Movement Patterns

1

2

Directions:

1–2. Identify the pattern. Extend the pattern by circling the movement that could come next.

3

4

5

6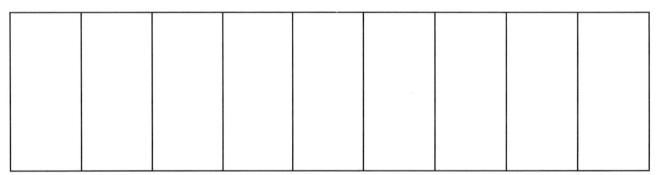

Copyright © Macmillan/McGraw-Hill, a division of The McGraw-Hill Companies, Inc.

Directions:

3–5. Extend the pattern by circling the movement that could come next.

6. Create a movement pattern. Show your pattern another way in the squares. Explain your pattern by acting it out.

Math at Home Activity: Create movement patterns and have your child copy your pattern. Then allow your child to make up his or her own pattern and watch to see if you can copy it correctly. Be sure to try AB, ABB, AAB patterns.

Chapter 3　Lesson 8

Predicting Patterns

If , then .

If , then .

1

If , then .

If , then .

2

If , then .

If , then .

Directions:
1. If the weather pattern continues what will you wear tomorrow? Circle it.
2. If the weather pattern continues what will you play tomorrow? Circle it.

3

If 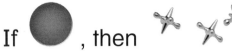, then  .

If , then  .

4

If 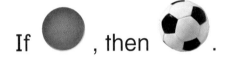, then .

If , then .

5

If , then  .

If 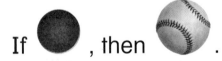, then .

Directions:

3–5. Every day Sam and Kim flip a counter to help them decide what to play. Each color stands for a different activity each day. If each pattern continues, what activity will they do next. Circle it.

Chapter 3   Lesson 9

D

A pattern is on the plate.
What pattern do you see?

Color the boxes to show the pattern another way. Explain.

FOLD DOWN

Problem Solving in Art

Real-World MATH

Patterns are everywhere!
Let's look in the kitchen.

This book belongs to

_____

A

Patterns are on the cup.
What patterns do you see?

Is there a pattern on me?

Patterns are on the table.
What patterns do you see?

Name _____

1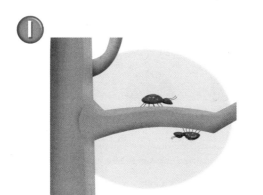

2

3

4

5

Directions:
1. Circle the bug that is above the branch. Put an X on the bug that is under the branch.
2. Circle the box that is on top. Put an X on the box that is in the middle. Underline the box that is on the bottom.
3. Circle the boat that is before the red boat. Put an X on the boat that is after the green boat.
4–5. Circle the picture that shows what could come next.

Chapter 3

Summative Assessment

Name _____

1

2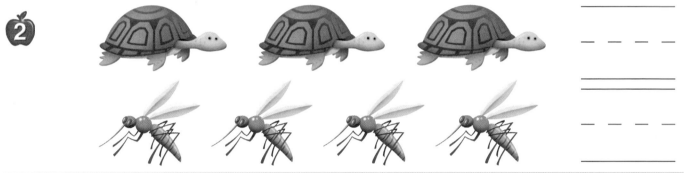

3

4

Directions:
1. Circle the shapes that are alike. Put an X on the shapes that are different.
2. Draw a line from each object in one row to an object in the row below. Count the objects in each row. Write the number. Put an X on the number and group that is more.
3. Look at the number on each dog. Color that many bones above the dog. Write the numbers in order from 0 to 5.
4. Count the animals. Write the number.

94   ninety-four

Formative Assessment

Name _____

1.

    ◯   ◯   ◯

2.

    ◯   ◯   ◯

3.

    ◯   ◯   ◯

4.

    ◯   ◯   ◯

Directions: Listen as your teacher reads each problem.
Choose the correct answer.

5.

◯   ◯   ◯

6.

◯   ◯   ◯

7.

4   5   6

◯   ◯   ◯

8.

◯   ◯   ◯

Directions: Listen as your teacher reads each problem.
Choose the correct answer.

Summative Assessment

Use Numbers to 10

Key Vocabulary

ordinal numbers

Explore

How many eggs do you see?

Math Online

Take the Chapter Readiness
Quiz at macmillanmh.com.

✓ Are You Ready for Chapter 4?

1

2

3

4

_____   _____

- - - - - - -   - - - - - - -

_____   _____

Directions:
1. Draw a line from each baseball to a baseball mitt.
2. Color 5 leaves green.
3. Circle the row with 4 nests.
4. Count the objects in each group. Write the number.
   Draw a circle around the group that has more.

This page checks skills needed for Chapter 4.

MATH at HOME

Dear Family,

Today my class started Chapter 4, **Use Numbers to 10**. I will be learning to count and order numbers to 10. Here are my vocabulary words, an activity we can do, and a list of books we can read together.

Love, _____

Activity

Count the types of clothes in a closet. You write the word and your child can write the number of items.

Key Vocabulary

ordinal numbers

first   second   third

Math Online Click on the eGlossary link at macmillanmh.com to find out more about these words. There are 13 languages.

Books to Read

Ten Flashing Fireflies
by Philemon Sturges
North-South Books,
1995.

Mouse Count
by Ellen Stoll Walsh
Voyager Books,
1995.

I Hunter
by Pat Hutchins,
Harper Collins
Publishers, 1986.

Estimada familia:

Hoy mi clase comenzó el Capítulo 4, **Usa los números hasta el 10**. A continuación, están mis palabras de vocabulario, una actividad que podemos realizar y una lista de libros que podemos leer juntos.

Cariños, _____

Actividad

Cuenten los tipos de ropa que hay en el armario. Ustedes escriben la palabra y su hijo(a) escribe el número de artículos.

Vocabulario clave

Números ordinales

primero segundo tercero

Math Online Visiten el enlace eGlossary en macmillanmh.com para averiguar más sobre estas palabras, las cuales se muestran en 13 idiomas.

Libros recomendados

¿Cómo cuentan hasta diez los dinosaurios?
de Jane Yolan and Mark Teague
Scholastic, 2004.

Cuenta ratones
de Ellen Stoll Walsh
Fondo de Cultura Economica
USA, 1996.

Uno, dos, tres
de Pat Mora,
Clarion Books, 2000.

Numbers 6 and 7

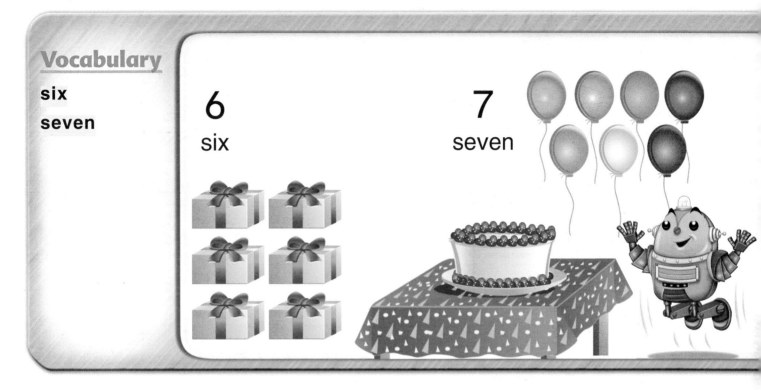

Vocabulary

six

seven

6

six

7

seven

①

②

Copyright © Macmillan/McGraw-Hill, a division of The McGraw-Hill Companies, Inc.

Directions:

1. Count the objects in the row. Say the number. Use color tiles to show how many objects. Draw a box around each bow.
2. Count the objects in the row. Say the number. Use color tiles to show how many objects. Draw a string for each balloon.

3

4

5

6

7

Directions:

3–7. Use color tiles to count the objects in each group. Say the number. Count and color one box for each object in that group.

 Math at Home Activity: Take a walk with your child. Find six and seven objects such as mailboxes or houses. Have your child count the objects.

Number 8

Vocabulary

eight

8 eight

Directions: Count the insects in each group. Use cubes to show how many insects.
Circle the groups of insects that show eight. Put an X on the groups that do not show eight.
Tell a classmate how many insects there are in each group.

①

②

③

 ④

Directions:

1–2. Circle the group that has eight objects.

3–4. Count the objects. Say the number.
Talk with a classmate to find out how many more you
should draw to make 8. Draw more to make a group of 8.

 Math at Home Activity: Draw a picture of a penny jar. Ask
your child to trace 8 pennies. Have your child color and cut the
pennies out and glue them on the jar. Count the pennies.

Read and Write 6, 7, and 8

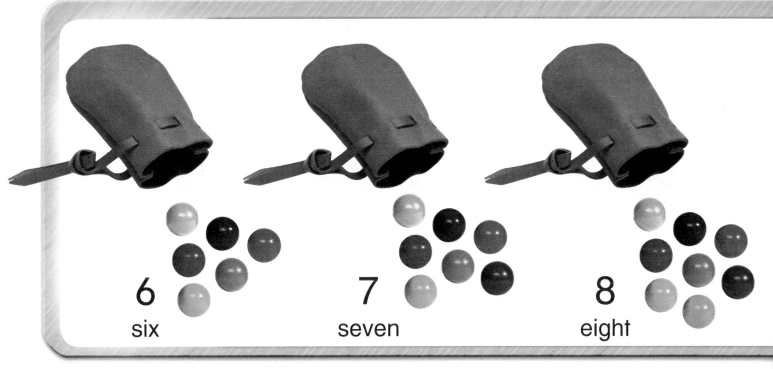

6
six

7
seven

8
eight

①

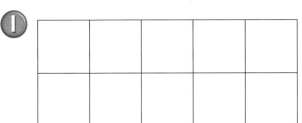

②

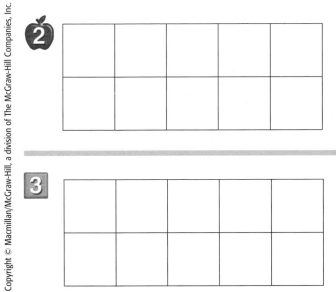

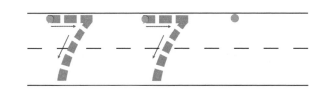

3

Directions:
1. Draw 6 marbles. Say the number. Trace and write the number.
2. Draw 7 marbles. Say the number. Trace and write the number.
3. Draw 8 marbles. Say the number. Trace and write the number.

Chapter 4   Lesson 3

one hundred five   105

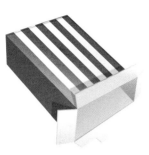

_____
_ _ _ _ _
_____

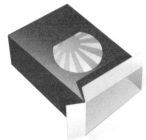

_____
_ _ _ _ _
_____

_____
_ _ _ _ _
_____

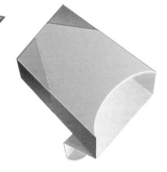

_____
_ _ _ _ _
_____

Directions:

4–7. Count the objects in each group. Say the number. Use WorkMat 5 and counters to show the number. Write the number.

Math at Home Activity: Using six index cards help your child make 2 cards with 6 dots, 7 dots, and 8 dots. Write each number. Play a matching game.

Name _____

1

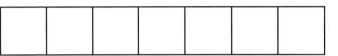

2

3

_____

- - - - - - -

_____

Directions:
1. Count the objects. Color one box for each object in that group.
2. Circle the groups of shoes that show eight. Put an X on the groups that do not show eight.
3. Count the objects. Write the number.

Surf's Up!
Counting

You Will Need

Play with a partner. Take turns.

- ○ Roll .
- ○ Move your that number of spaces.
- ○ Take a counter each time you land on a surfboard.
- ○ When you reach finish, count your counters.
- ○ The winner has the most counters.

start

finish

Numbers 9 and 10

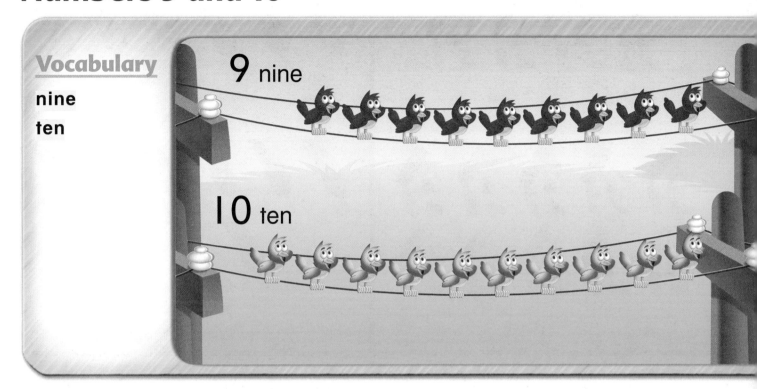

Vocabulary

nine

ten

9 nine

10 ten

Directions:

1–2. Count the objects in each group. Say the number. Use counters to show how many objects. Draw a red circle around the group with nine objects. Draw a blue circle around the group with ten objects.

3

4

5

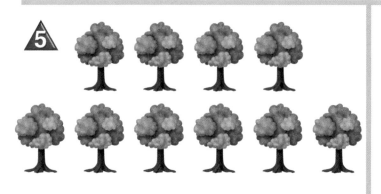

6

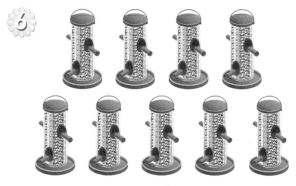

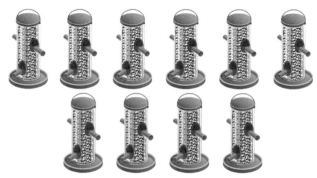

Directions:

3–6. Count the objects in each group. Say the number. Draw a red circle around the group of nine. Draw a blue circle around the group of ten.

Math at Home Activity: Use two different colored sheets of paper. Tear each sheet into 12 pieces. Ask your child to count out 9 pieces of one color and 10 pieces of the other color.

Name _____

Read and Write 9 and 10

9
nine

10
ten

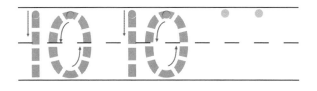

Directions:
1–2. Count the objects. Say the number. Trace and write the number.

3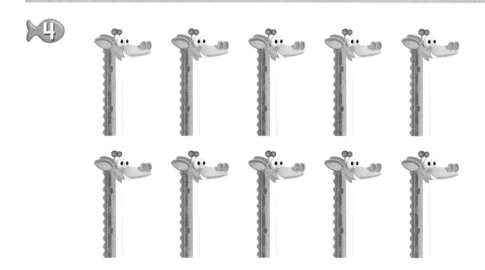

_____

– – – – – – – – – –

_____

4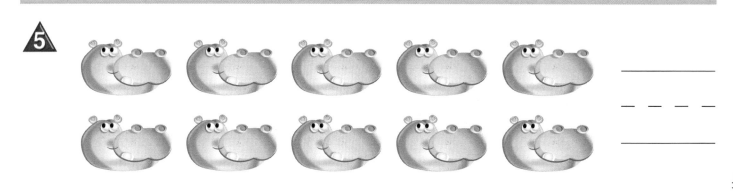

_____

– – – – – – – – – –

_____

5

_____

– – – – – – – – – –

_____

6

_____

– – – – – – – – – –

_____

Directions:

3–6. Count the animals. Say the number. Use WorkMat 5 and counters to show the number. Write the number.

 Math at Home Activity: Use a book with numbered pages. Ask your child to count the pages to page nine and write nine. Then count pages to 10 and write 10.

Name _____

Problem-Solving Strategy
Draw a Picture

How many are at the circus?

8   9

Directions:
1–2. Look at the picture. Find a group of objects that has
     the number shown. Draw those objects.

3

🐟4

10

7

🔺5

✿6

9

6

Copyright © Macmillan/McGraw-Hill, a division of The McGraw-Hill Companies, Inc.

Directions:
3–6. Look at the picture. Find a group of objects that
has the number shown. Draw those objects.

Math at Home Activity: Take advantage of problem-solving
opportunities during daily routines such as riding in the car,
bedtime, doing laundry, putting away groceries, planning
schedules, and so on.

Chapter 4　Lesson 6

Compare Numbers to 10

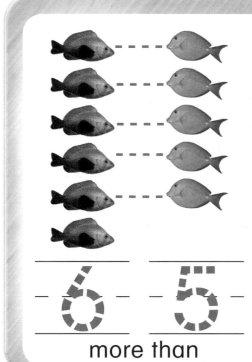 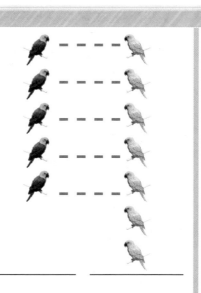 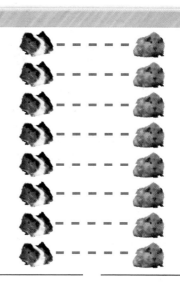

6	5				
more than	less than	same number as			

①   _ _ _ _ _ _ _

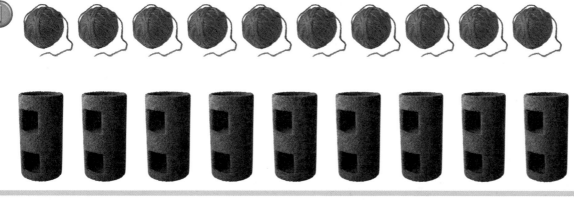

②   _ _ _ _ _ _ _

Directions:
1–2. Count how many objects are in each group. Write the numbers. Draw lines to match objects in one group with objects in the other. Circle the number and group that has more. Put an X on the number and group that has less. Put a box around the number and groups if there are the same number in each group.

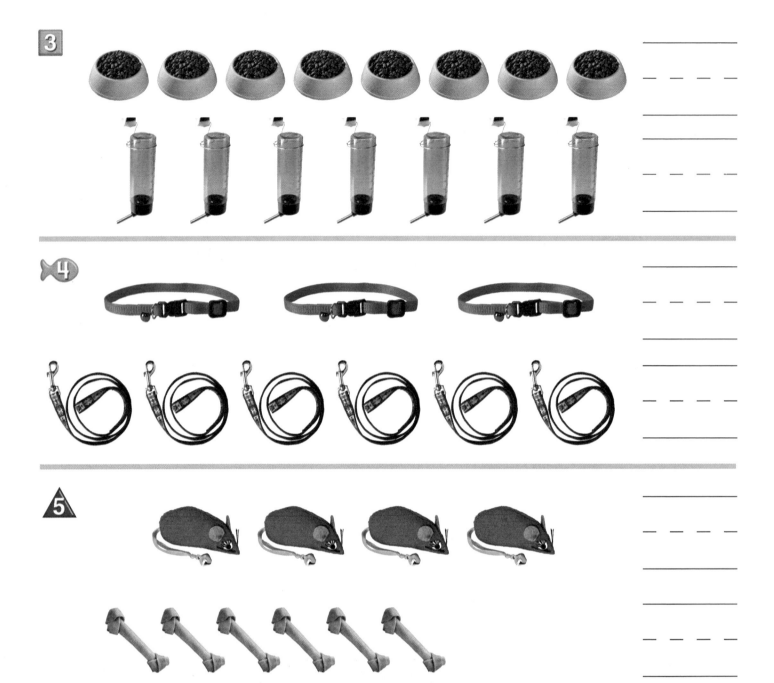

3
_____

_____

_____

4
_____

_____

_____

_____

5
_____

_____

_____

_____

6
_____

_____

_____

_____

Directions:

3–6. Count how many objects are in each group. Write the numbers. Draw lines to match objects in one group with objects in the other. Circle the number and group that are more. Put an X on the number and group that are less. Put a box around the number and groups if there are the same number in each group.

Math at Home Activity: Make two different groups of 10 items or less. Ask your child which group has more, less, or if they have the same number of items. Write the number.

Name _____

Order Numbers to 10

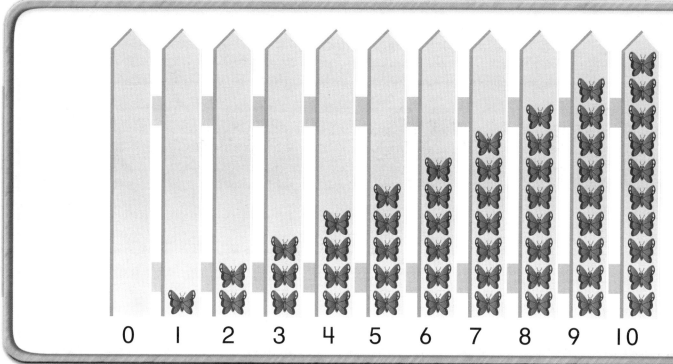

0 1 2 3 4 5 6 7 8 9 10

1

0 1 2 3 ___

2

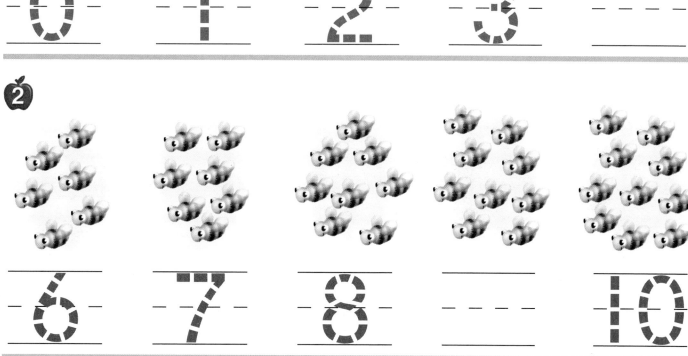

6 7 8 ___ 10

Directions:

1–2. Count the objects. Trace the numbers. Write the missing number that comes just before or just after.

Chapter 4   Lesson 8

one hundred seventeen   117

3

  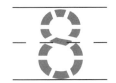 

 4

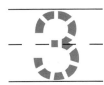 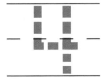 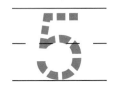 

 5

 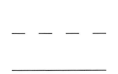 

 6

Directions:

3–4. Count the seeds and circles on the objects. Trace the numbers. Write the missing number that comes before or after.

5–6. Count the boxes and petals on the objects. Write the missing numbers that come before and after. Draw the missing items on the object.

 Math at Home Activity: Cut small squares. Ask your child to number them one to 10. Shuffle. Ask your child to order them. Count again.

Chapter 4 Lesson 8

Ordinal Numbers

Vocabulary

ordinal numbers

Directions:

1. Draw a circle around the first rabbit. Put an X on the third rabbit. Underline the fifth rabbit.
2. Draw a circle around the second duck. Put an X on the fourth duck. Underline the seventh duck.

Directions: Name the position of each vulture. Circle the sixth vulture. Put an X on the third vulture Name the position of each snake. Circle the first snake. Name the position of each lizard. Put an X on the seventh lizard.

Math at Home Activity: Line up a row of ten stuffed animals or toys all facing the same direction. Have your child tell you which animal is first, sixth, tenth, and fourth.

Nests are in a tree.

Winter

How many nests do you see?

I see _____ nests.

FOLD DOWN

Problem Solving
in Science

Spring

Real-World MATH

There are lots of things on trees.
Take a look. What do you see?

This book belongs to

_____

Birds are in the tree.

Autumn

How many birds do you see?

I see _____ birds.

Apples are on the tree.

Summer

How many apples do you see?

I see _____ apples.

Name _____

1

‌ _____

2

‌ _____

3

‌ _____

‌ _____

4

__0__   __1__   __2__   _____

Directions:
1–2. Count the objects. Write the number.
3. Count how many objects are in each group. Write the number.
   Draw lines to match objects in one group with objects in the other.
   Put an x on the number and row that are less.
4. Count the objects. Write the missing number that comes after.
   Draw the missing drum sticks to show the number.

Chapter 4   one hundred twenty-three   **123**

Spiral Review Chapters 1–4

Name _____

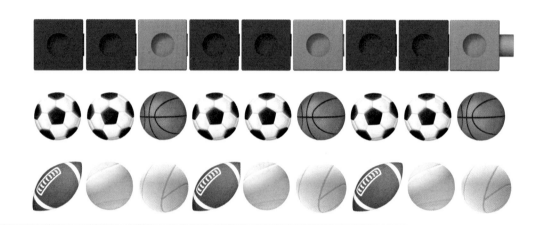

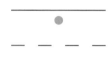

Directions:

1. Compare the patterns. Circle the pattern that matches the pattern shown with the cubes.
2. Write how many children are playing soccer.
3. Circle the flowers that are in a group of five. Put an X on the flowers that are in a group of four.

124   one hundred twenty-four

Name _____

1.

8

 ⬭    ⬭    ⬭

2.

3

2   1   4
⬭   ⬭   ⬭

3.

 ⬭    ⬭    ⬭

4.

2

1   3   4
⬭   ⬭   ⬭

Copyright © Macmillan/McGraw-Hill, a division of The McGraw-Hill Companies, Inc.

Directions: Listen as your teacher reads each problem.
Choose the correct answer.

5.

6   7   8
◯   ◯   ◯

6.

◯   ◯   ◯

7.

◯   ◯   ◯

8.

Directions: Listen as your teacher reads each problem. Choose the correct answer.

Summative Assessment

Construct and Use Graphs

Key Vocabulary

data

real graph

picture graph

Explore

What is this picture showing?

Are there more red handprints or blue handprints?

Name _____

Are You Ready for Chapter 5?

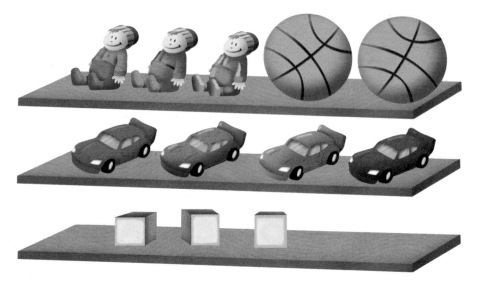

1

2

3

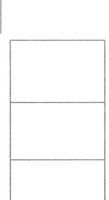

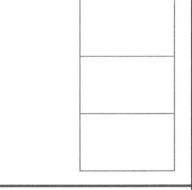

4

_____

_ _ _ _ _ _ _

_____

_____

_ _ _ _ _ _ _

_____

Directions:
1. Color one box for each doll to show how many dolls.
2. Color one box for each block to show how many blocks.
3. Color one box for each ball to show how many balls.
4. Count the bears in each group. Write the number. Circle the group that has more.

This page checks skills needed for Chapter 5.

Dear Family,

Today my class started Chapter 5, **Construct and Use Graphs**. I will be learning to make and read graphs. Here are my vocabulary words, an activity we can do, and a list of books we can read together.

Love,

_____

Activity

Have your child ask family members if their favorite juice is orange, grape, or apple. Record their answers on a graph. Ask your child questions about the information on the graph. Have your child ask you questions about the data on the graph.

Key Vocabulary

data

Favorite Foods	
Food	Votes
🍎	ＩＩＩＩＩ
🍌	ＩＩＩ
🥔	ＩＩＩＩＩ ＩＩＩ

real graph graph using real objects

picture graph

Our Favorite Pets					
🐱 Cats	🐱	🐱			
🐶 Dogs	🐶	🐶	🐶	🐶	
🐟 Fish	🐟				

Math Online > Click on the eGlossary link at macmillanmh.com to find out more about these words. There are 13 languages.

Books to Read

Tiger Math: Learning to Graph from a Baby Tiger
by Ann Whitehead Nagda
Henry Holt & Company, 2002.

The Best Vacation Ever
by Stuart J. Murphy
Harper Trophy, 1997.

Anno's Flea Market
by Mitsumasa Anno
Penguin Group Incorporated, 1984.

Estimada familia:

Hoy mi clase comenzó el Capítulo 5, **Construye y usa gráficas**. Aprenderé a hacer y a leer gráficas. A continuación, están mis palabras de vocabulario, una actividad que podemos realizar y una lista de libros que podemos leer juntos.

Cariños, _____

Actividad

Inventen sondeos para su familia. Por ejemplo, pídanle a su hijo(a) que les pregunte a sus parientes si su jugo favorito es el jugo de naranjas, uvas o manzanas. Anoten sus respuestas en una gráfica. Háganle preguntas a su hijo(a) acerca de la información en la gráfica. Pídanle a su hijo(a) que les haga preguntas acerca de los datos en la gráfica.

Vocabulario clave

Datos

Comidas Favoritas	
Comida	Votos
🍎	ℍℍ
🍌	ℍℍ
🥜	ℍℍ ℍℍℍ

Gráfica real Una gráfica que usa objetos reales.

Pictograma

Nuestros animales domésticos favorito					
Gatos					
Perros					
Pescados					

Math Online Visiten el enlace eGlossary en macmillanmh.com para averiguar más sobre estas palabras, las cuales se muestran en 13 idiomas.

Libros recomendados

¿Hagamos una grafia?
de Lisa Trumbauer
Yellow Umbrella Books, 2005.

Más máthematicas con los chocolates de m&m's
de Barbara Barbieri McGrath
Charlesbridge Publishing, 2001.

Name _____

Collect and Record Data

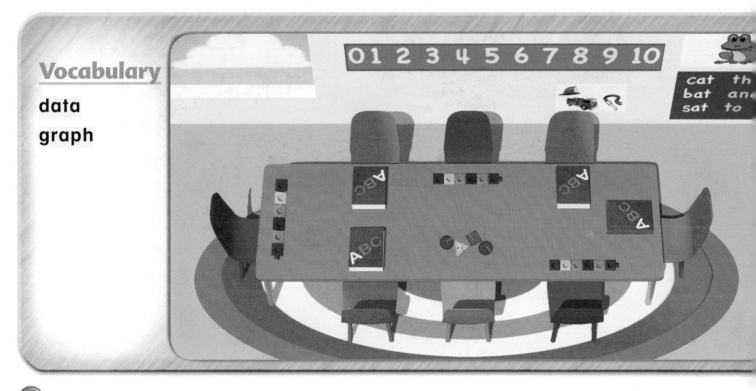

Vocabulary

data

graph

①

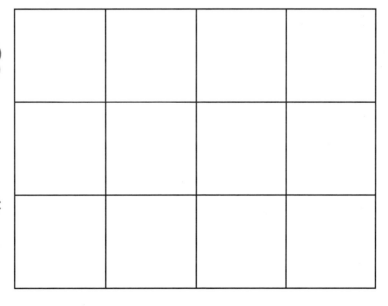

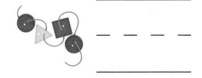 _____

 _____

 _____

 _____

Directions:

1. Place a yellow color tile on the graph for each cube train. Place a red color tile on the graph for each book. Place a green color tile on the graph for each necklace. Color the boxes to match. Write the number.

Chapter 5   Lesson 1   one hundred thirty-one   131

  _____

 _____

 _____

Directions:

2. Place a green color tile on the graph for each car. Place a yellow color tile on the graph for each bus. Place a red color tile on the graph for each bike. Color the boxes to match. Write the number.

Math at Home Activity: Draw a picture of some of the items in a kitchen cupboard. Color boxes to show how many of each item. Write the number of each.

Chapter 5   Lesson 1

Name _____

Real Graphs

Copyright © Macmillan/McGraw-Hill, a division of The McGraw-Hill Companies, Inc.

Vocabulary

real graph

Directions: Use red and blue color tiles to make a picture on the easel. Sort your tiles by color. Put them on the graph. Tell about the graph. Which group has more tiles? Circle it.

Directions: Use yellow and green color tiles to make a picture on the chalkboard. Sort your tiles by color. Put them on the graph. Tell about the graph. Which group has less tiles? Circle it.

Math at Home Activity: Toss nine pennies. Sort heads and tails. Graph results as shown above. Tell which has more and which has less.

Name _____

Problem-Solving Strategy

Look for a Pattern

What do you see?

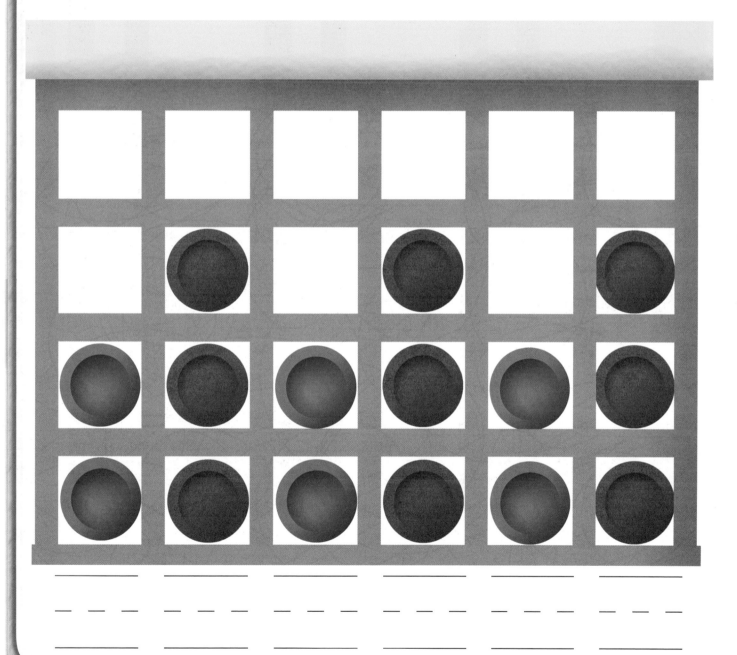

_____

_____

_____

Directions: Write the number of checkers in each column on the lines below the graph. Discuss the pattern of numbers and colors.

Directions: Create an AB pattern by coloring a different number of windows in each building. Have a partner write the numbers that show how many windows you colored in each building. Discuss the pattern of numbers and colors.

Math at Home Activity: Take advantage of problem-solving opportunities during daily routines such as riding in the car, bedtime, doing laundry, putting away groceries, planning schedules, and so on.

136 one hundred thirty-six

Chapter 5   Lesson 3

Name _____

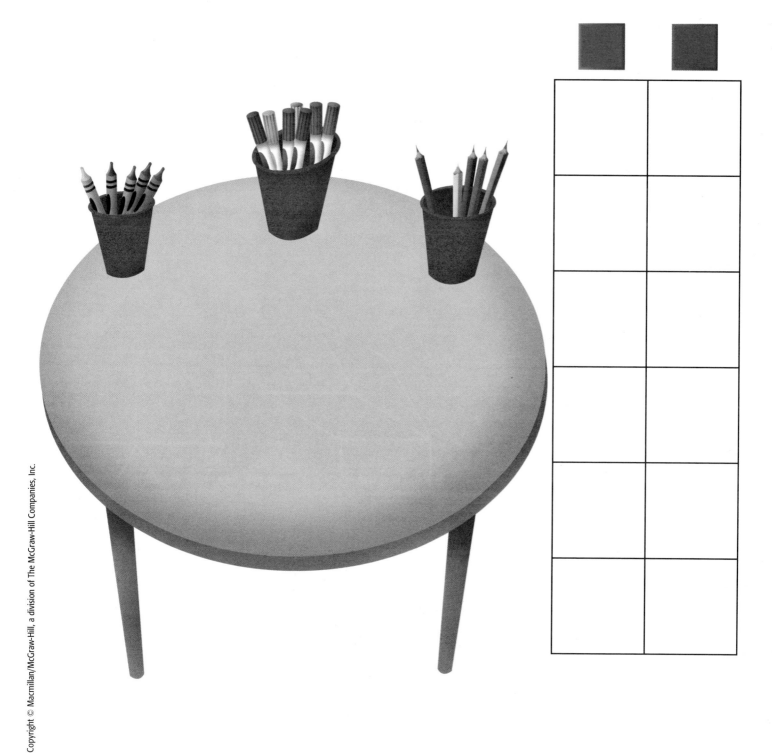

Directions: Use color tiles to make a picture on the table. Sort your tiles by color.
Put them on the graph. Which group has more tiles? Circle it.

Chapter 5   one hundred thirty-seven   137

Boat Building
Graphing

Play with a partner. Take turns.
- Choose one boat each.
- Build the boat using pattern blocks.
- Graph the figures you used to build your boat by coloring the boxes.
- Count to see who used more of each figure.

You Will Need

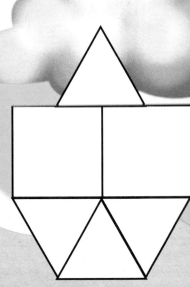

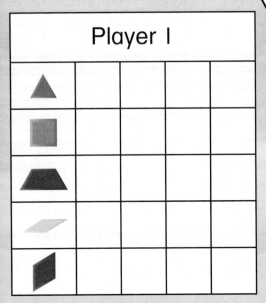

Player 1

Player 2

Name _____

Picture Graphs

Vocabulary

picture graph

Which pet do you like more?

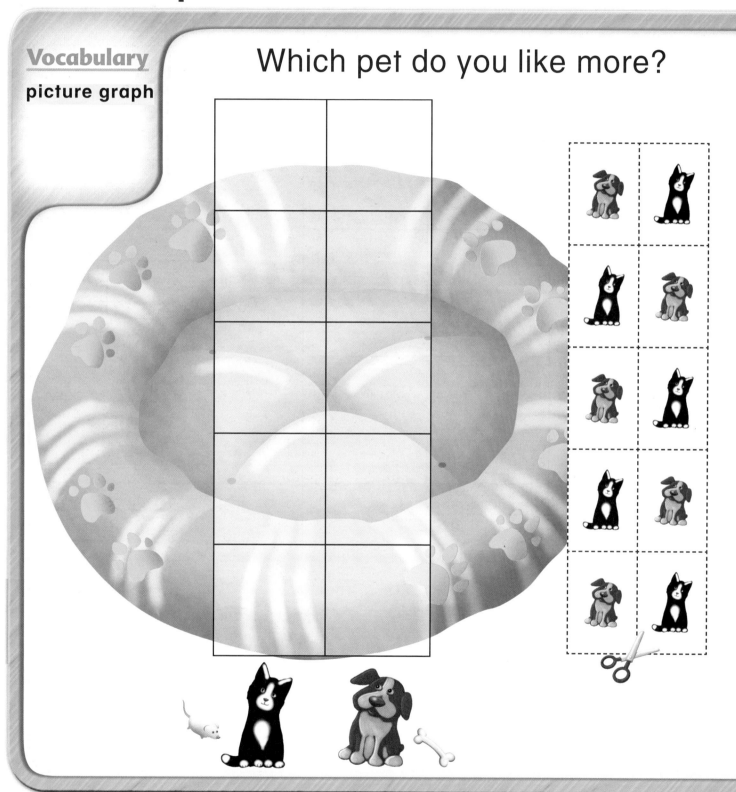

Directions: Ask five students which pet they would rather have. Cut and glue the picture of the pet on the graph. Which group has more pets? Circle it. Talk with a classmate about your graph.

Where do you like to swim?

Directions: Ask five students if they would rather swim at the beach or in a pool. Cut and glue the picture each student chose on the graph. Which group has less places? Circle it. Talk with a classmate about your graph.

Math at Home Activity: Gather toys such as dominos and cars. Sort the toys into two groups. Make a picture graph of the toys. Circle the group that shows more.

Make a Graph

Vocabulary

survey

What is your favorite color?

Directions: Ask five students this question: which of these colors–red, green, yellow, blue, or orange–is your favorite color? Use that color crayon to color one of the crayons in the dashed boxes. Cut and paste the dashed boxes on the graph. Talk with a classmate about your Graph.

_____

- - - - - - - - - - - -

How many _____ do you have?

5					
4					
3					
2					
1					

Directions: Decide on a question. Fill in the blank. Ask five students to answer the question. Fill in the graph to show their answers.

Math at Home Activity: Cut red and blue circles from paper. Ask family members which color is their favorite. Make a picture graph with the circles. Which color do people like the most?

Chapter 5   Lesson 5

What is your favorite 4th of July activity? Ask 5 students.

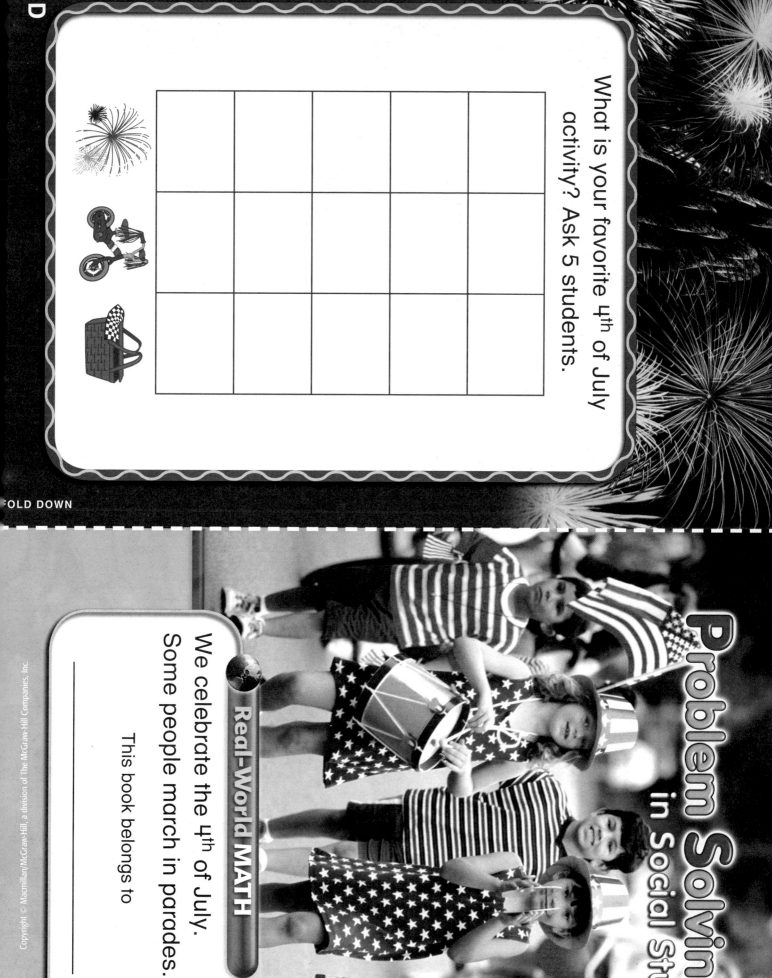

FOLD DOWN

Problem Solving in Social Studies

Real-World MATH

We celebrate the 4th of July. Some people march in parades.

This book belongs to

_____

Here is a graph. It shows what Juan's friends like to do on the 4ᵗʰ of July.

Which has the most votes? Explain.

Some people have picnics.

Name _____

 _ _ _ _ _ _ _ _   _ _ _ _ _ _ _ _   _ _ _ _ _ _ _ _

Directions: Place a red color tile on the graph for each baseball. Place a green color tile on the graph for each mitt. Place a yellow color tile on the graph for each bat. Color the boxes to match. Write the number. Which object has more? Circle it. Which object has less? Put an X on it.

Chapter 5

Spiral Review Chapters 1–5

Name _____

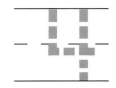   

Directions:

1. Count each object. Color a square for each object counted. Write the number.
2. Count the spots. Trace the numbers. Write the missing number that comes just before or just after. Draw the missing spots to show the number.
3. Circle the object that could come next in the pattern.

146   one hundred forty-six

Name _____

1.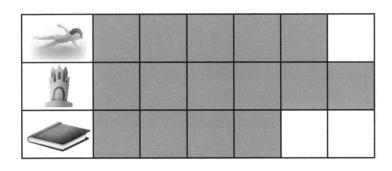

⃝   ⃝

⃝

2.

⃝   ⃝   ⃝

3.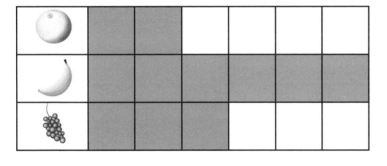

⃝   ⃝

4.

9

8   9   10

⃝   ⃝   ⃝

Directions: Listen as the teacher reads each problem. Choose the correct answer.

Chapter 5   one hundred forty-seven   **147**

5.

◯   ◯   ◯

6.

12   10   9

◯   ◯   ◯

7.

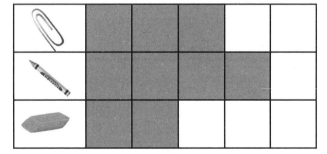      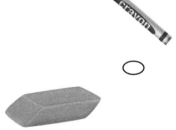

                         ◯   ◯

                              ◯

8.

◯   ◯   ◯

Directions: Listen as the teacher reads each problem. Choose the correct answer.

Summative Assessment

Use Numbers to 20

> Key Vocabulary
> **twenty**

Explore
Draw a circle on the puppets with hats and a box on the puppets without hats.
Are there more puppets with hats or puppets without hats?

Name _____

 Are You Ready for Chapter 6?

①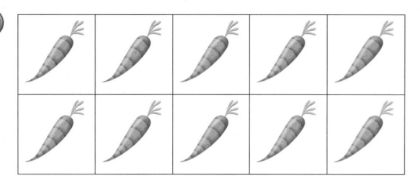

_____

②

_____   _____   _____

③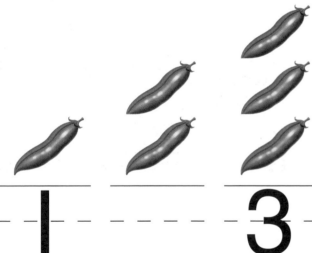

| 1 | ___ | 3 |

④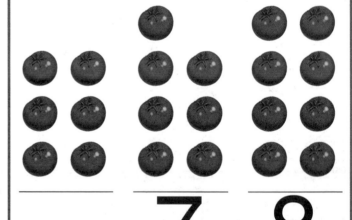

___ | 7 | 8

Directions:
1. Count the carrots. Write the number.
2. Count the ears of corn in each group. Write the number.
3-4. Write the missing number.

This page checks skills needed for Chapter 6.

MATH at HOME

Dear Family,

Today my class started Chapter 6, **Use Numbers to 20**. I will be learning to count and order numbers to 20. Here is my vocabulary word, an activity we can do, and a list of books we can read together.

Love, _____

Activity

Have your child find 20 or less of an object. For example, have your child find 13 pennies or 17 crayons. Count the objects. Write the number. Compare to show more, less, or the same amounts.

Key Vocabulary

twenty

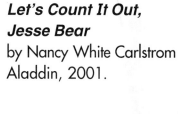

20

2 tens

Math Online ▷ Click on the eGlossary link at <u>macmillanmh.com</u> to find out more about these words. There are 13 languages.

Books to Read

Gathering: A Northwoods Counting Book
by Betsy Bowen
Houghton Mifflin Company, 1999.

Let's Count It Out, Jesse Bear
by Nancy White Carlstrom
Aladdin, 2001.

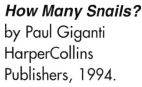

How Many Snails?
by Paul Giganti
HarperCollins Publishers, 1994.

MATEMÁTICAS en CASA

Estimada familia:

Hoy mi clase comenzó el Capítulo 6, **Usa los números hasta el 20**. Aprenderé a contar y a ordenar los números hasta el 20. A continuación, está mi palabra de vocabulario, una actividad que podemos realizar y una lista de libros que podemos leer juntos.

Cariños,

_____

Vocabulario clave

veinte

20

2 decenas

Math Online Visiten el enlace eGlossary en macmillanmh.com para averiguar más sobre estas palabras, las cuales se muestran en 13 idiomas.

Actividad

Hagan que su hijo(a) busque 20 ó menos de un objeto. Por ejemplo, pídanle que busque 13 monedas de 1¢ ó 17 crayones. Cuenten los objetos. Escriban el número. Comparen para mostrar más, menos o cantidades iguales.

Libros para leer

El libro de contar de los chocolates marca m&m
de Barbara Barbieri McGrath
Charlesbridge
Publishing, 1996.

Cuenta con el beisbol
de Barbara Barbieri McGrath
Charlesbridge Publishing, 2005.

152   one hundred fifty-two

Numbers 11 and 12

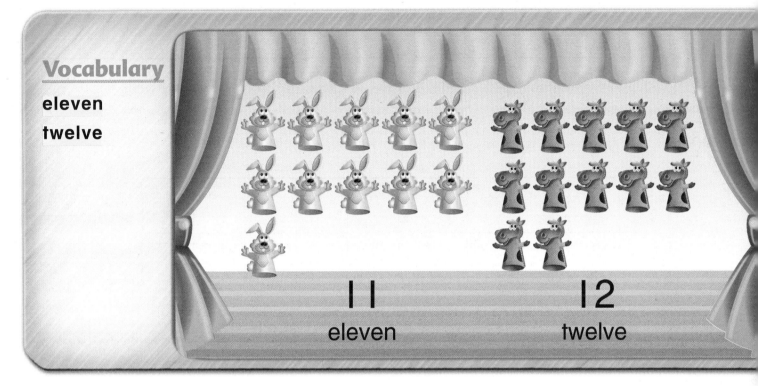

Vocabulary

eleven

twelve

11
eleven

12
twelve

 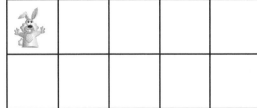 

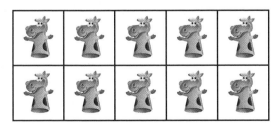 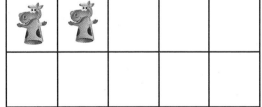 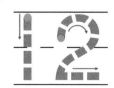

Directions:
1–2. Count the objects. Say the number. Use WorkMat 6 and counters to show the number. Trace the number.

3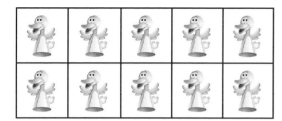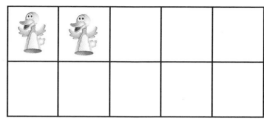

_____

- - - - -

4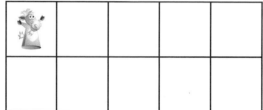

_____

- - - - -

5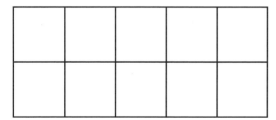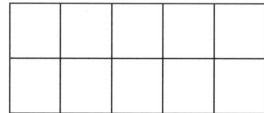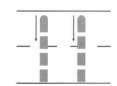

6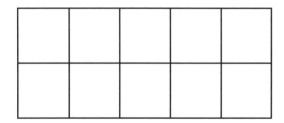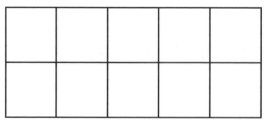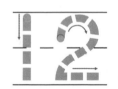

Directions:
3–4. Count the objects. Say the number. Use WorkMat 6 and counters to show the number. Write the number.
5–6. Trace the number. Say the number. Use Workmat 6 and counters to count the number. Using the ten-frame above, draw circles for counters to show the number.

 Math at Home Activity: Use an empty egg carton. Ask your child to fill each egg holder with one item. Use the items to count 11 and 12. Write each number.

Numbers 13, 14, and 15

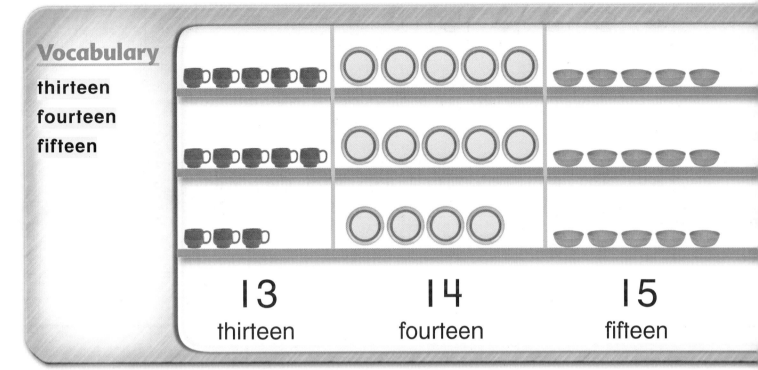

Vocabulary

thirteen

fourteen

fifteen

13
thirteen

14
fourteen

15
fifteen

1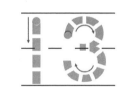

2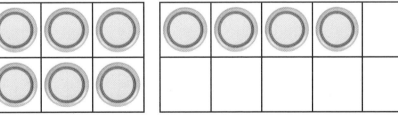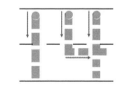

3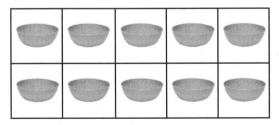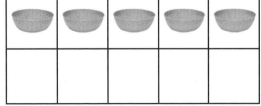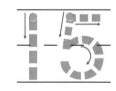

Directions:

1–3. Count the objects. Say the number. Use WorkMat 6 and counters to show the number. Trace the number.

4

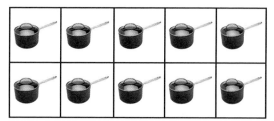 

_____
- - - -

5

_____
- - - -
_____

6

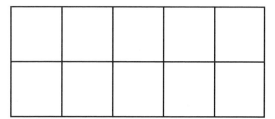 

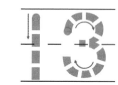

7

 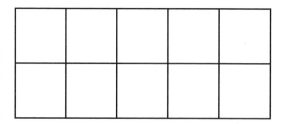

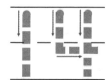

Directions:

4–5. Count the objects. Say the number. Use WorkMat 6 and counters to show the number. Write the number.

6–7. Trace the number. Say the number. Use WorkMat 6 and counters to count the number. Using the ten-frame above, draw circles for counters to show the number.

Math at Home Activity: Have your child draw dots to make groups of 13, 14, and 15 and count the dots in each group. Then ask your child to write the numbers.

156   one hundred fifty-six

Chapter 6   Lesson 2

Numbers 16 and 17

Vocabulary

sixteen

seventeen

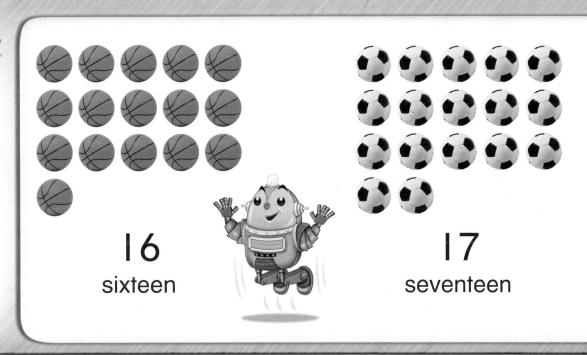

16
sixteen

17
seventeen

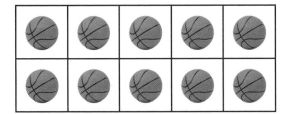  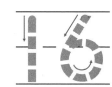

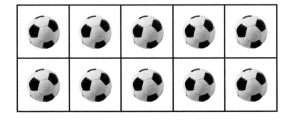 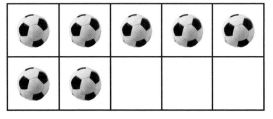 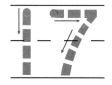

Directions:

1–2. Count the objects. Say the number. Use WorkMat 6
and counters to show the number. Trace the number.

3

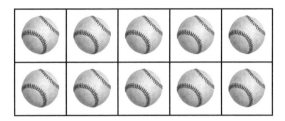 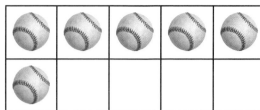

_____
- - - - -
_____

4

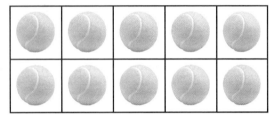 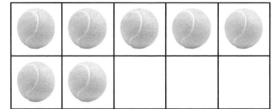

_____
- - - - -
_____

5

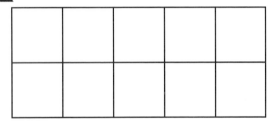 

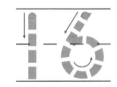

6

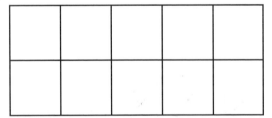 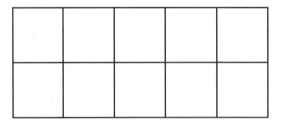

Directions:

3–4. Count the objects. Say the number. Use WorkMat 6 and counters to show the number. Write the number.

5–6. Trace the number. Say the number. Use WorkMat 6 and counters to count the number. Using the ten-frame above, draw circles for counters to show the number.

 Math at Home Activity: Ask your child to make groups of 16 and 17 using dry macaroni. Have your child show how each group has 10 and 6 or 7 more and then write 16 and 17.

Chapter 6   Lesson 3

Name _____

1  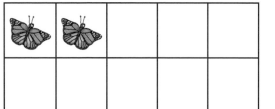 _____

2 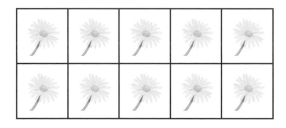 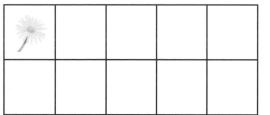 _____

3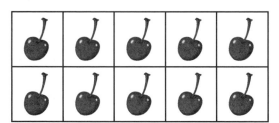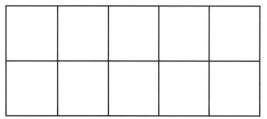

4

Directions:
1–2. Count the objects. Write the number.
3. Draw more cherries to make 14.
4. Draw more leaves to make 17.

Leap Frog!

Recognizing Numbers to 17

Play with a partner. Take turns.
- Put your cubes on **Start**. Roll the [5].
- Move your cube that many spaces.
- If you land on another player's cube, or on a frog, you may "leap" over it to the next space.
- The first player to 17 wins.

You Will Need

Problem-Solving Strategy
Look for a Pattern

How many?

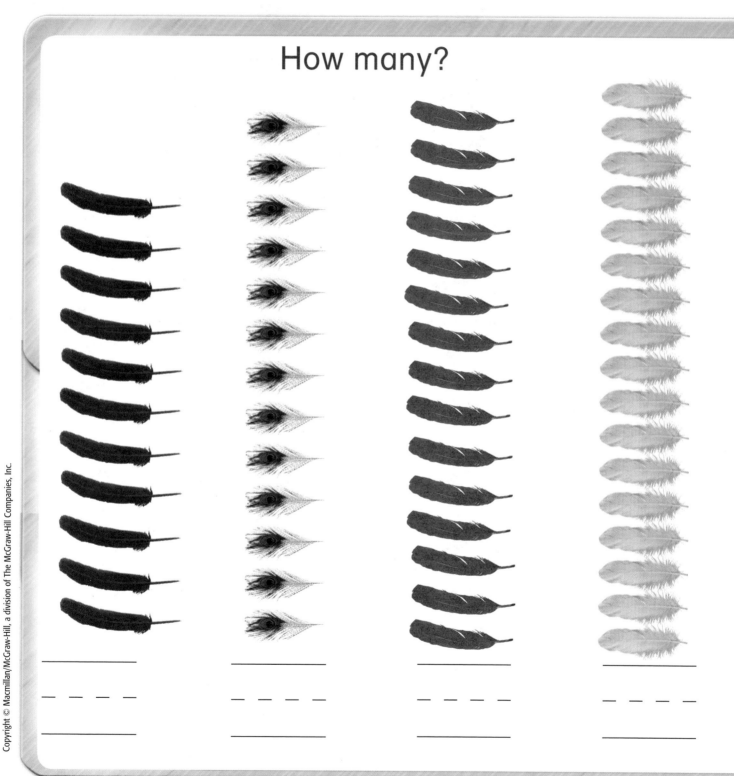

_____   _____   _____   _____

_ _ _ _ _ _ _ _ _ _

_____

Directions:
Count the feathers. Write the number. What pattern do you notice in the numbers?

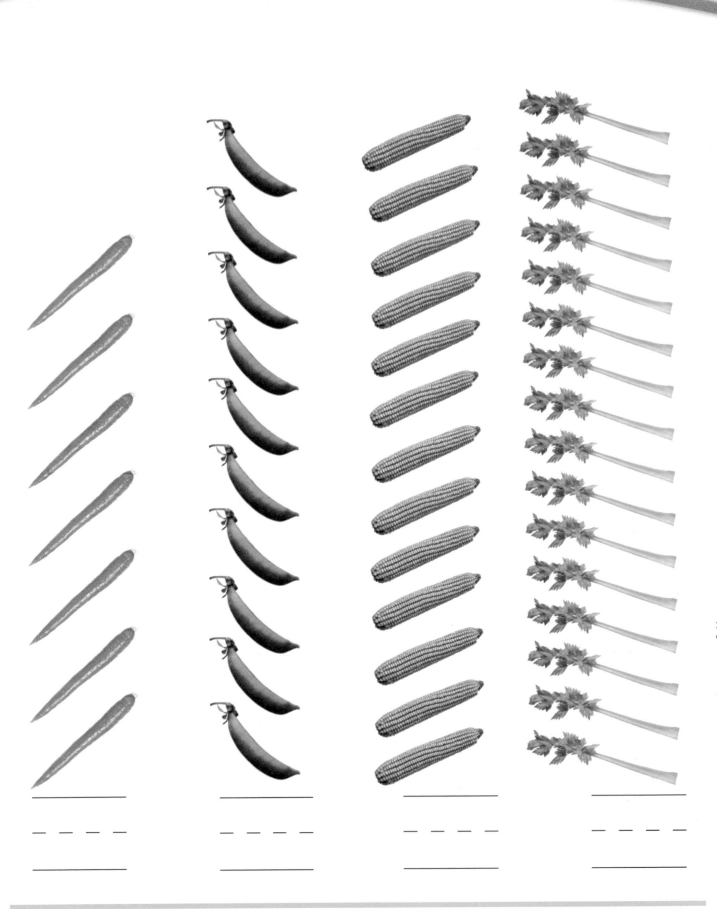

_____

- - - - - - -

_____

Copyright © Macmillan/McGraw-Hill, a division of The McGraw-Hill Companies, Inc.

Directions:
Count the vegetables. Write the number.
What pattern do you notice in the numbers?

 Math at Home Activity: Take advantage of problem-solving opportunities during daily routines. When on a walk help your child count and record the number of cars and trucks he or she sees. Discuss how this data could be displayed.

162   one hundred sixty-two

Numbers 18, 19, and 20

Vocabulary

eighteen

nineteen

twenty

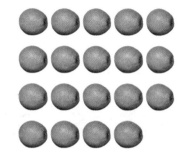

18	19	20
eighteen	nineteen	twenty

 1

  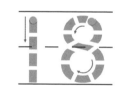

 2

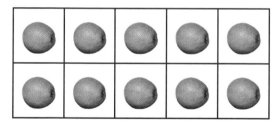 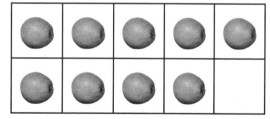 

 3

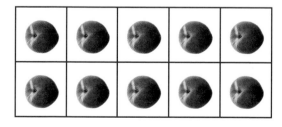 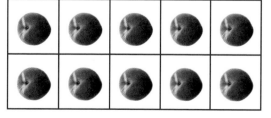 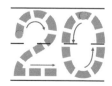

Directions:

1–3. Count the objects by counting on from 10. Say the number.
Use WorkMat 6 and counters to show the number. Trace the number.

_____
- - - - -
_____

_____
- - - - -
_____

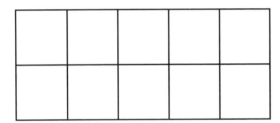 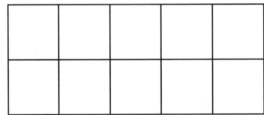

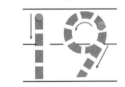

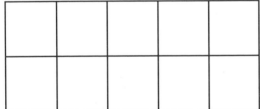 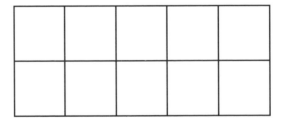

Directions:

4–5. Count the objects. Say the number. Use WorkMat 6 and counters to show the number. Write the number.

6–7. Trace the number. Say the number. Use WorkMat 6 and counters to count the number. Draw circles for counters to show the number.

 Math at Home Activity: Draw a piggy bank on paper. Count coins in groups of 18, 19, and 20. Place a group of coins on the piggy bank. Write the number. Repeat for other numbers.

164   one hundred sixty-four

Chapter 6   Lesson 5

Compare Numbers to 20

more than   less than   same number

_____ _____

_____ _____

Directions:

1–2. Count the objects. Write the number. Draw an X through the number that describes the group with more objects.

3

_____

- - - - -   - - - - -

_____

4

_____

- - - - -   - - - - -

_____

5

- - - - -   - - - - -

_____

6

8   10

Directions:

3–5. Count the objects. Write the number. Circle the number that shows less. Put a box around the numbers that are the same.

6. Draw circles on each plate to show the number. Circle the number that shows less.

 Math at Home Activity: Make groups of buttons with various amounts to 20. Ask your child to count the buttons and tell which group has more, less, or is the same number.

Chapter 6   Lesson 6

Name _____

Order Numbers to 20

0 1 2 3 4 5 6 7 8 9 10 11 12 13 14 15 16 17 18 19 20

1

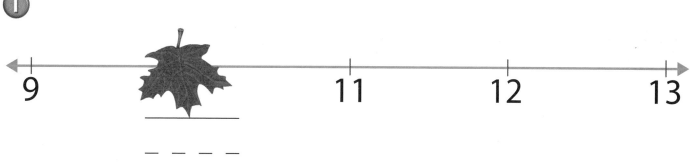

9 _____ _____ 11 _____ 12 _____ 13

_____

- - - - -

_____

2

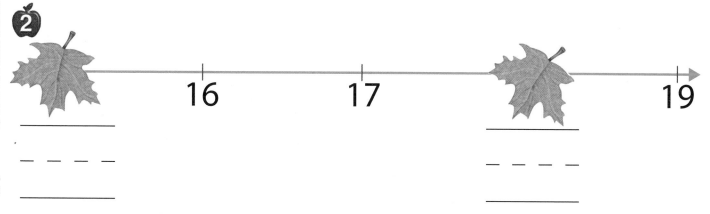

_____ 16 _____ 17 _____ 19

_____   _____

- - - - -   - - - - -

_____   _____

Directions:
1–2. Write the missing number(s).

3

11   12      14   _____

_ _ _ _

_____

4

   15   16   _____   18

_ _ _ _

_____

5

_____   9   10   _____   12

_ _ _ _

_____

6

16      18   19

_____

_ _ _ _

_____

 Math at Home Activity: Cut squares and number them from 0 to 20. Show any five numbers in number order. Hide one number. Ask your child which number is missing.

There are postcard collections.

GRAND CANYON
GREETINGS FROM

Statue of Liberty, NY

SPACE NEEDLE
SEATTLE

YELLOWSTONE NATIONAL PARK

Welcome to the Alamo

...e Bridge

How many postcards are here?

_____ postcards

Problem Solving
in Social Studies

Real-World MATH

Some people have collections.
A collection is many of the same
kind of thing.

This book belongs to

_____

There are coin collections.

How many coins are here?

_____ coins

C

There are stamp collections.

How many stamps are here?

_____ stamps

B

Name _____

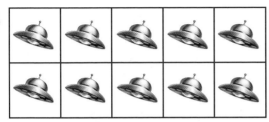 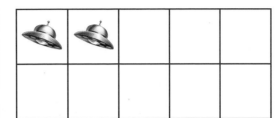

_____

_____

3

_____

 _____    _____

16   19

_____   _____

Directions:
1–3. Count the objects. Write the number.
4. Count the objects in each group. Write the number.
   Circle the group that has more.
5. Write the hidden numbers.

Chapter 6   one hundred seventy-one   171

Name _____

1

2

3

Directions:
1. Circle the object that could come next in the pattern.
2. Draw lines to match objects in one group with objects in the other. Write the number. Circle the number and group that are more.
3. Count the fish, star fish, and crabs. Write the number.

Name _____

1.

16   18   19
◯   ◯   ◯

2.

◯   ◯   ◯

3.

◯   ◯   ◯

4.

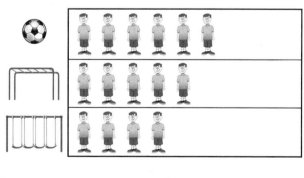

4   5   6
◯   ◯   ◯

Directions: Listen as the teacher reads each problem. Choose the correct answer.

5.

      ◯   ◯   ◯

6.

      19   18   16

      ◯   ◯   ◯

7.

      ◯   ◯   ◯

8.

      ◯   ◯   ◯

Directions: Listen as the teacher reads each problem. Choose the correct answer.

174   one hundred seventy-four

Summative Assessment

Compare Measurements

Key Vocabulary

length

weight

capacity

area

temperature

Explore

Draw an X on the elephant that is bigger.

Draw a circle around the elephant with the shorter trunk.

Name _____

Are You Ready for Chapter 7?

①

②

③

④

Directions:
1. Circle the pencil that is longer.
2. Circle the quilt that covers more of the bed.
3. Circle the one that can carry more people.
4. Circle the animal you could hold in your hand.

This page checks skills needed for Chapter 7.

Dear Family,

Today my class started Chapter 7, **Compare Measurements**.
I will be learning about length, weight, capacity, area, and
temperature. Here are my vocabulary words, an activity we can do,
and a list of books we can read together.

Love,

_____

Activity

Help your child find objects that differ in length such as pencils, crayons, shoe laces, and silverware. Have your child choose two objects and decide which one is longer. Find objects of differing weight. Have your child choose two objects and decide which one is lighter.

Key Vocabulary

length

holds more the pitcher holds more than the glass

holds less the glass holds less than the pitcher

Math Online Click on the eGlossary link at macmillanmh.com
to find out more about these words. There are 13 languages.

Books to Read

The Best Bug Parade
by Stuart J. Murphy
HarperCollins Publishers,
1996.

**Super Sand Castle
Saturday**
by Stuart J. Murphy
HarperCollins Publishers,
1999.

Length
by Henry Pluckrose
Scholastic Library
Publishing, 1995.

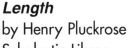

MATEMÁTICAS en CASA

Estimada familia:

Hoy mi clase comenzó el Capítulo 7, **Compara medidas**. Aprenderé sobre la longitud, el peso, la capacidad, area, y temperature. A continuación, están mis palabras de vocabulario, una actividad que podemos realizar y una lista de libros que podemos leer juntos.

Cariños, _____

Actividad

Ayuden a su hijo(a) a encontrar objetos que difieran en longitud, como lápices, lápices de colores, cordones de zapatos y cubiertos. Pídanle a su hijo(a) que seleccione dos objetos y decida cuál es el más largo. Busquen objetos de diferentes pesos. Pídanle a su hijo(a) que seleccione dos objetos y que decida cuál es el más liviano.

Vocabulario clave

longitud

contiene más la jarra contiene más que el vaso

contiene menos el vaso contiene menos que la jarra

Math Online > Visiten el enlace eGlossary en <u>macmillanmh.com</u> para averiguar más sobre estas palabras, las cuales se muestran en 13 idiomas.

Libros recomendados

Medir: la casita perfecta
de John Burstein
Gareth Stevens Publishing, 2006.

¿Por qué medimos?
de Lisa Trumbauer
Red Brick, 2006.

Compare Length

Vocabulary

length
longer
shorter
same as

Directions:

1. Use cubes to make a train shorter than the fish. Draw the train above the fish.
   Use cubes to make a train longer than the fish. Draw the train below the fish.

2

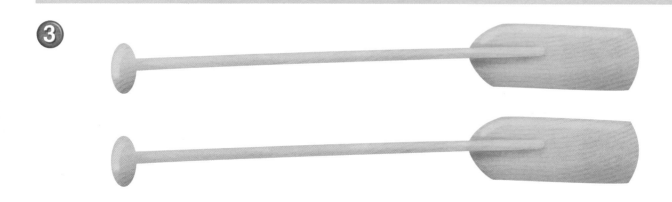

3

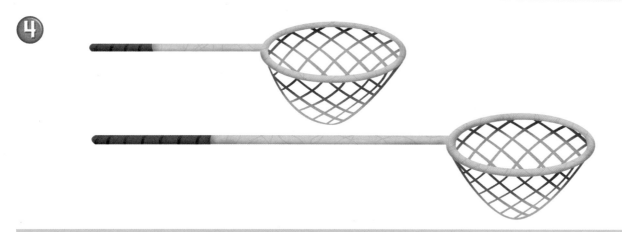

4

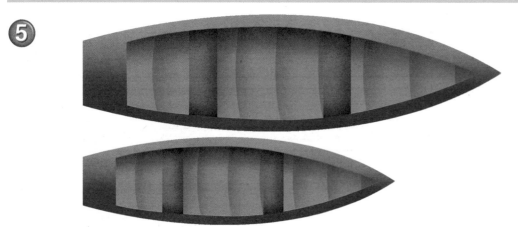

5

Directions:

2–5. For each set of pictures, compare the objects and put an X on the object that is shorter. Circle the object that is longer. If the objects are the same length underline them.

Math at Home Activity: Place a spoon and pencil, or straw and crayon on a table, one above the other. Have your child tell which is longer and which is shorter.

Chapter 7   Lesson 1

Name _____

Order Length

Vocabulary

shortest

longest

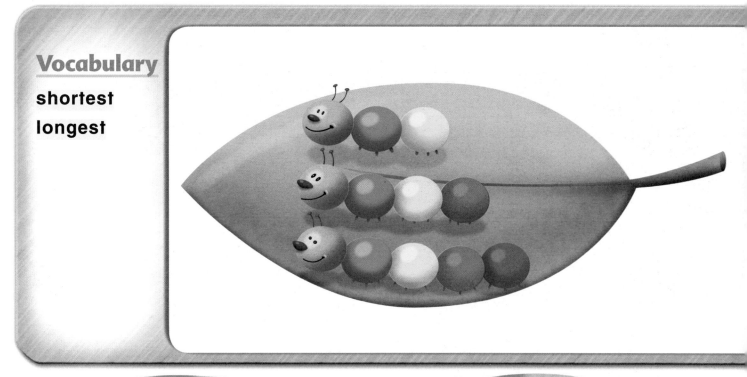

①

Directions:

1. Place 3 counters on the top twig. Trace the counters to make a caterpillar the same length as the twig.
   Place 4 counters on the middle twig. Trace the counters to make a caterpillar the same length as the twig.
   Place 5 or more counters on the bottom twig. Trace the counters to make a caterpillar the same length as
   the twig. Tell which caterpillar is the shortest and which caterpillar is the longest.

2

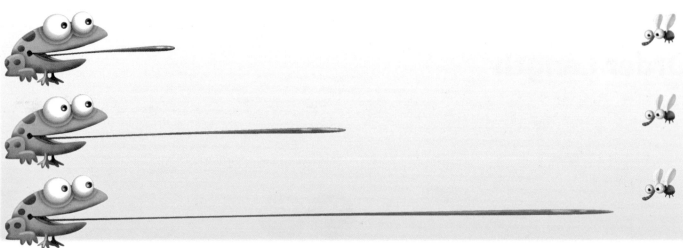

3

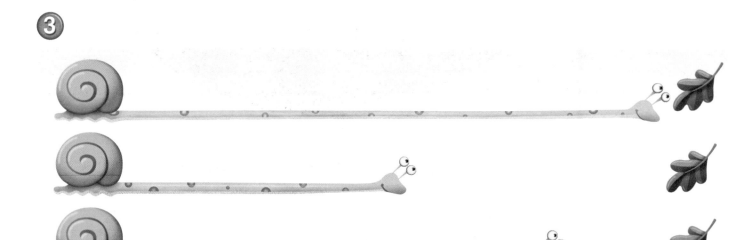

4

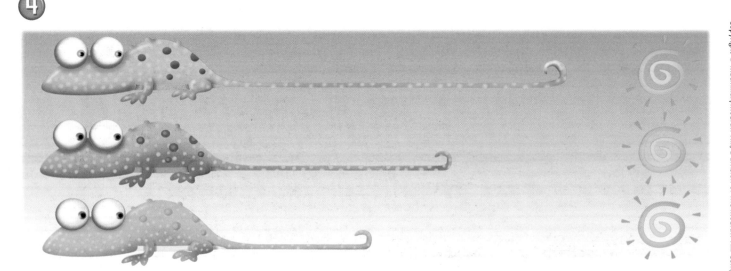

Directions:

2–4. Put a green X on the group of objects that is in order from shortest to longest. Put a blue X on the group of objects that is in order from longest to shortest. Put a red X on the group of objects that is not in order of length.

 Math at Home Activity: Cut string into three strips of different lengths. Ask your child to order the strips from shortest to longest and from longest to shortest.

182   one hundred eighty-two

Chapter 7   Lesson 2

Compare Weight

Vocabulary

weight
heavier
lighter
equal to

(1)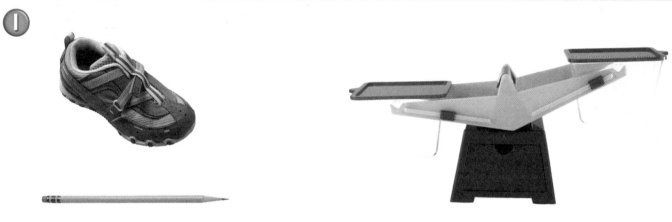

(2)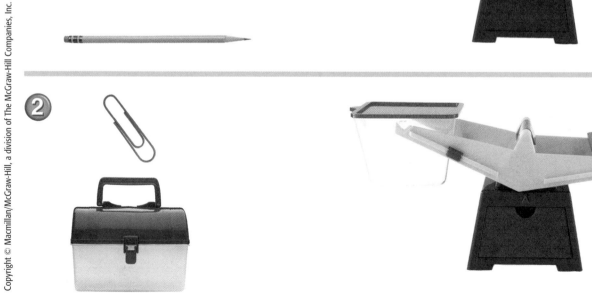

Directions:

1–2. Compare the objects. Draw a line from each object to the place on the balance
scale that shows its weight.

③

 ④

⑤

⑥

⑦

⑧

Directions:

3–6. Compare the objects. Circle the heavier object. Put an X on the lighter object. If the objects weigh the same underline them.
7. Draw an object that is heavier than scissors.
8. Draw an object that is lighter than a chair.

 Math at Home Activity: Use a canned good and empty cup. Ask your child to close his or her eyes. Place one item in each of your child's hands. Ask your child which hand holds the heavier item and which hand holds the lighter item.

Name _____

Problem-Solving Strategy
Guess and Check

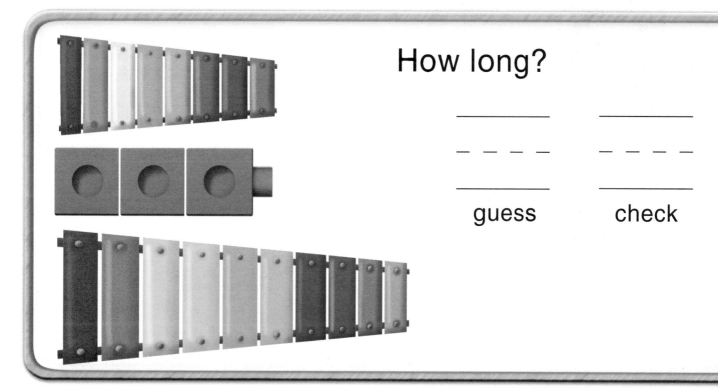

How long?

_____   _____
- - - - - - -   - - - - - - -
_____   _____
guess   check

1

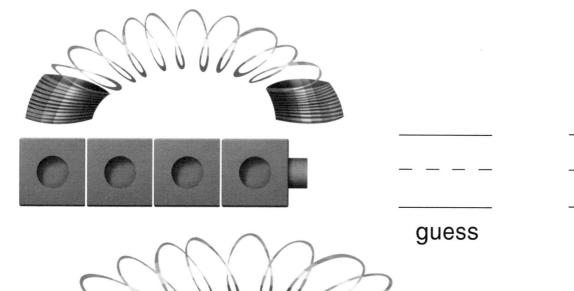

_____   _____
- - - - - - -   - - - - - - -
_____   _____
guess   check

Directions:

1. Compare the objects. Circle the object that is longer. Then guess how many cubes long the longer object is. Is your answer close? Use cubes to check.

②

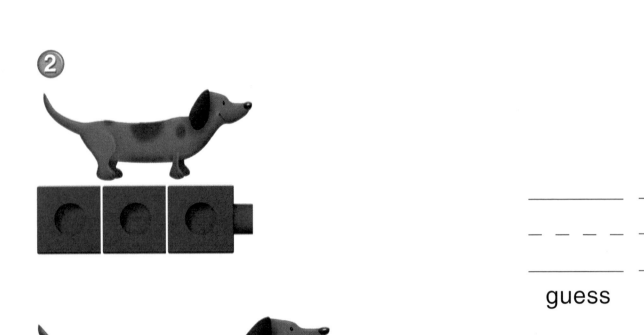

_____ _____

- - - - - - - - -

_____ _____

guess   check

③

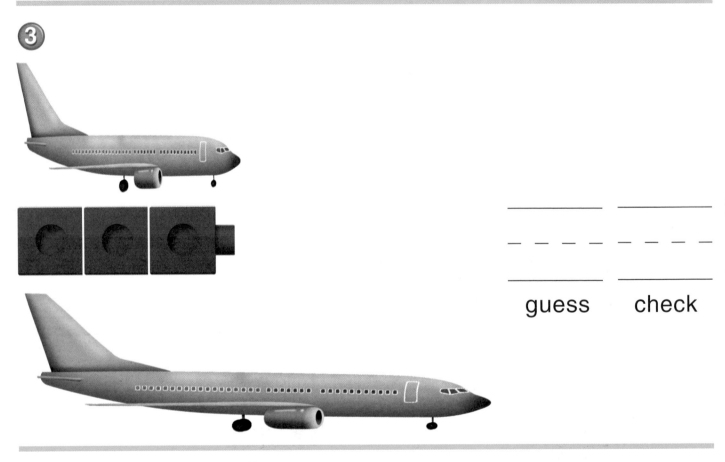

_____ _____

- - - - - - - - -

_____ _____

guess   check

Directions:

2–3. Compare the objects. Circle the object that is longer. Then guess how many cubes long the longer object is. Is your answer close? Use cubes to check your guess.

Math at Home Activity: Take advantage of problem-solving opportunities during daily routines such as riding in the car, bedtime, doing laundry, putting away groceries, planning schedules, and so on.

Name _____

①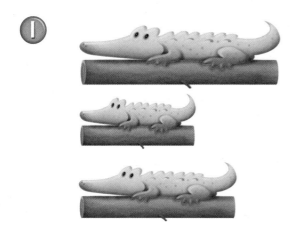

②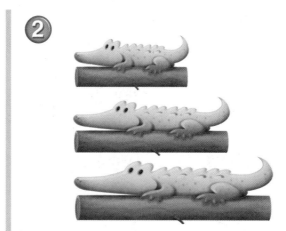

③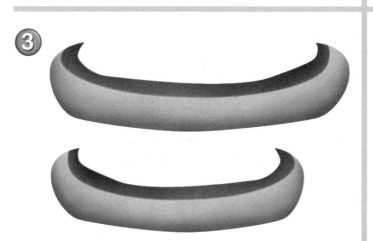

④

⑤

⑥

Directions:
1–2. Put a green X on the group of objects that are lined up from shortest to longest.
Put a red X on the group of objects that are not lined up from shortest to longest.
3. Circle the canoe that is longer. Put an X on the canoe that is shorter.
4–6. Circle the object that is heavier. Put an X on the object that is lighter. If the objects weigh the same underline them.

Building a Snake
Comparing Length

You Will Need

48

Play with a partner. Take turns.
- Roll the 🎲.
- Move your ⚪ that number of spaces.
- Collect the number of cubes shown on the space.
- Build a snake using the cubes.
- When you both reach **Finish**, compare the lengths of your snakes.
The longer snake wins.

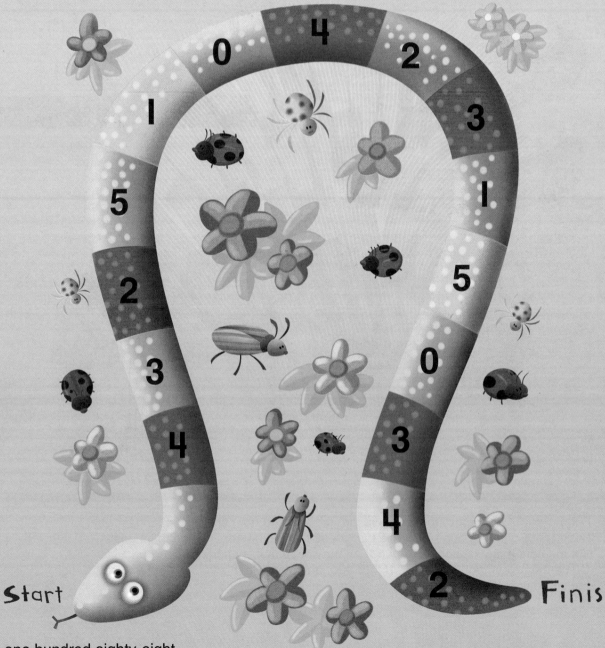

Compare Capacity

Copyright © Macmillan/McGraw-Hill, a division of The McGraw-Hill Companies, Inc.

Vocabulary

capacity
holds more
holds less
holds the same

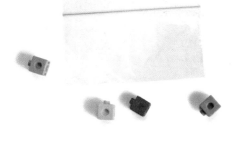

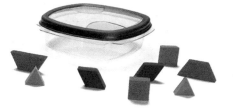

Directions:
1–2. Compare the containers. Circle the object that holds more.
Put an X on the object that holds less.

6

Directions:

3–6. Compare the containers. Circle the object that holds more. Put an X on the object that holds less. If the objects hold the same, underline them.

Math at Home Activity: Use a small empty bowl and a large empty bowl. Have your child fill the small bowl with dry pasta. Pour the pasta from the small bowl into the large bowl. Ask your child which holds more.

190   one hundred ninety

Chapter 7   Lesson 5

Name _____

Compare Area

Vocabulary

area
covers more
covers less
covers the
 same

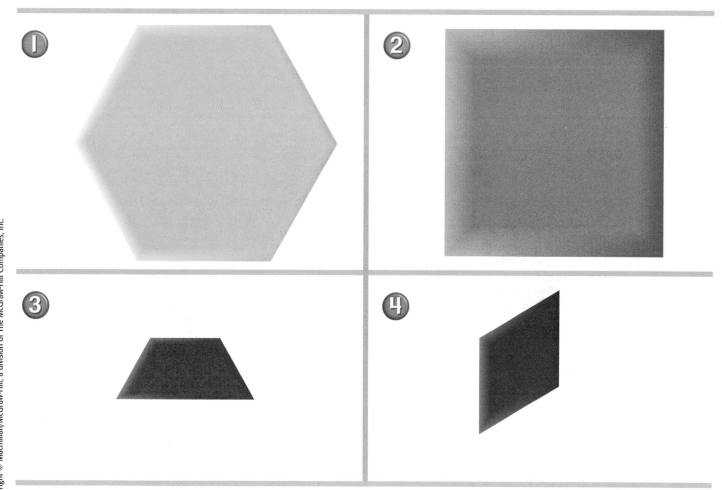

① ② ③ ④

Directions:

1–4. Place the matching pattern block on each figure. If the pattern block covers
 more area than the figure, circle the figure. If the pattern block covers less area
 than the figure, put an X on the figure. If the pattern block covers the same amount
 of area as the figure, underline the figure.

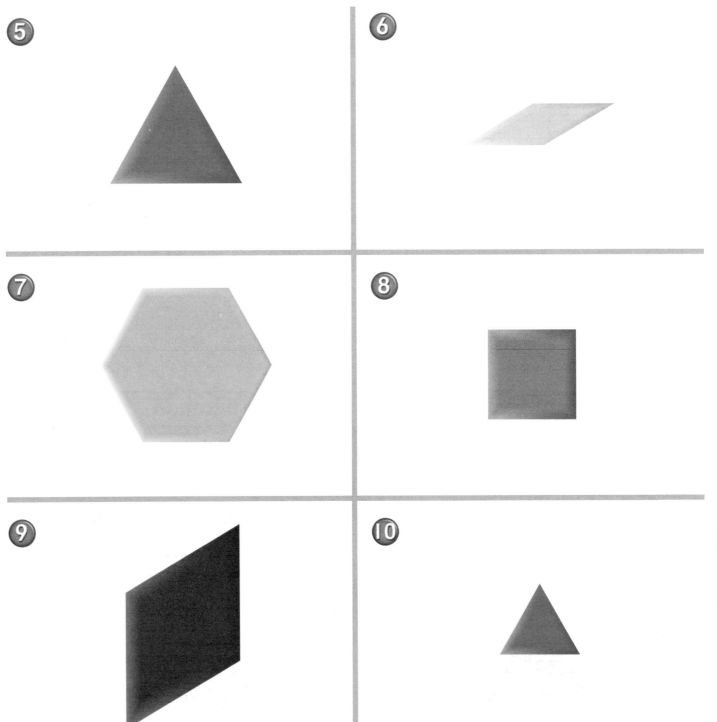

Directions:

5–10. Place the matching pattern block on each figure above. If the pattern block covers more area than the figure, circle the figure. If the pattern block covers less area than the figure, put an X on the figure. If the pattern block covers the same amount of area as the figure, underline the figure.

 Math at Home Activity: Use an object, such as a book, and have your child determine if other objects around the house cover more, less, or the same area as the object.

Chapter 7   Lesson 6

Name _____

Compare Temperature

Copyright © Macmillan/McGraw-Hill, a division of The McGraw-Hill Companies, Inc.

Vocabulary

hot

cold

temperature

Cold

Hot

 ①

 ②

 ③

Directions:

1. Compare. Circle the picture that shows hot.
2. Compare. Circle the object that is cold.
3. Compare. Name each object in the row. Circle the two objects that are about the same temperature.

Chapter 7   Lesson 7

one hundred ninety-three   **193**

Directions:
4. Compare. Circle the situation that is hot.
5. Compare. Circle the situation that is cold.
6. Compare. Circle the two situations that are about the same temperature.

Math at Home Activity: At dinner have your child name something he or she is eating that is hot and something he or she is eating that is cold.

D

What is your favorite flower?

_____

It may have grown
from a seed!

FOLD DOWN

Problem Solving
in Science

Real-World MATH

There are many types of flowers.

This book belongs to

_____

A

Which is the tallest? Circle your answer. Explain.

C

Some flowers grow from seeds.

Plant them. Watch them grow!

B

Name _____

1

2

3

4

Directions:
1. Circle the object that is longer.
2. Put an X on the object that is heavier.
3. Put an X on the object that holds more.
4. Circle the object that is colder.

Chapter 7

Spiral Review Chapters 1–7

Name _____

_____

- - - - -

_____

_____
- - - -
_____

_____
- - - -
_____

Directions:
1. Count the objects. Write the number.
2. Describe the colored figure in the box. Circle the figures in the group that are like the figure in the box. Put an X on the figures that are different than the figure in the box.
3. Count the green buttons on the clown suits. Write the number.

198 one hundred ninety-eight

Name

1.

    ◯   ◯   ◯

2.

    ◯   ◯   ◯

3.

    ◯   ◯   ◯

4. 15

    ◯   ◯   ◯

Directions: Listen as the teacher reads each problem.
Choose the correct answer.

5.

○   ○   ○

6.

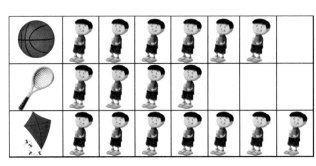

7   6   4

○   ○   ○

7.

○   ○   ○

8.

○   ○   ○

Directions: Listen as the teacher reads each problem.
Choose the correct answer.

Student Handbook

Built-In Workbook

Reference

How to Use the Student Handbook

Use the Student Handbook:

- when you need more practice writing numbers

- when you need to know the meaning of a math word

- when you need to find number patterns, to order numbers, or to skip count

- when you need help writing the number names

Glossary/Glosario

English	A	Español

about (page 218)

How many? about 20

aproximadamente

¿Cuántos? aproximadamente 20

above (page 71)

above

sobra

sobra

add (page 281)

3 ducks   2 more join   5 ducks in all

sumar

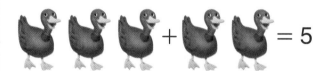

3 patos   2 más se unen   5 patos en total

after (page 75)

6 is just after 5

después

5 6 7 8

El 6 viene inmediatamente después del 5

Glossary/Glosario

English	A	Español

afternoon (page 229)

tarde

alike (same) (page 17)

alike   different

igual

igual   diferente

area (page 191)

covers more   covers less

área

cubre más   cubre menos

Glossary/Glosario

English		Español
before (page 75)	**B**	**antes**

6 is just before 7

El 6 viene inmediatamente antes del 7

below (page 71)

below

debajo

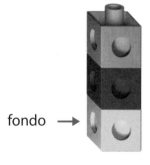

debajo

bottom (page 73)

bottom →

fondo

fondo →

C

calendar (page 233)

calendario

Glossary/Glosario

English	**Español**

capacity (page 189)

holds more   holds less

capacidad

contiene más   contiene menos

---

circle (page 259)

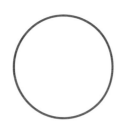

círculo

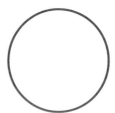

---

cold (page 193)

frío

---

cone (page 255)

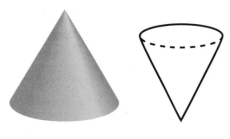

cono

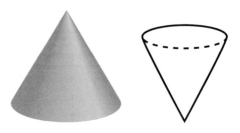

Glossary/Glosario

| **English** | | **Español** |

corner (page 261)

corner

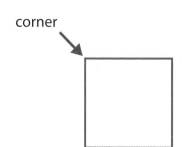

esquina

esquina

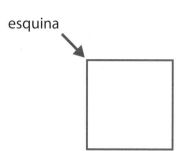

count (page 43)

| 1 | 2 | 3 |
| one | two | three |

contar

| 1 | 2 | 3 |
| uno | dos | tres |

covers less (page 191)

cubre menos

covers more (page 191)

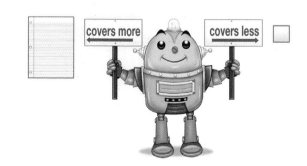

cubre más

Glossary/Glosario

English		Español

covers the same (page 191)   **C**   **cubre la misma cantidad**

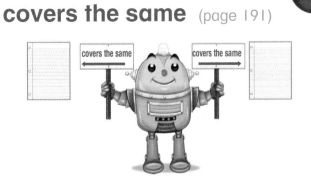 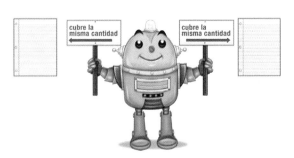

cube (page 255)

 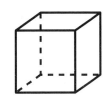

cubo

 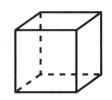

cylinder (page 255)

 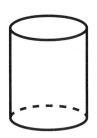

cilindro

D

data (page 131)

Favorite Foods	
Food	Votes
🍎	ⅲⅲ
🍌	ⅲ
🥪	ⅲⅲ ⅲ

information

datos

Comidas Favoritas	
Comida	Votos
🍎	ⅲⅲ
🍌	ⅲ
🥪	ⅲⅲ ⅲ

datos

Glossary/Glosario

<table>
<tr><th>English</th><th></th><th>Español</th></tr>
</table>

D

different (page 17)

different   alike

diferente

diferente   iguales

E

equal to (page 183)

 =

grupos iguales

3 en cada grupo

equal parts (page 269)

partes iguales

estimate (page 218)

How many? about 20

estimado

¿Cuántos? aproximadamente 20

Glossary/Glosario

English		Español
English	**E**	**Español**

evening (page 229)   atardecer

F

figure (page 255)   figura

G

graph (page 131)   gráfica

Our Favorite Sports
Soccer
Basketball
Baseball

Nuestros Deportes Favoritos
futbol
balón
beisbol

H

half (page 269)   mitad

half

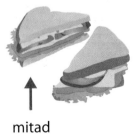

mitad

G8   Glossary

Glossary/Glosario

English	H	Español

heavy (heavier, heaviest)
(page 183)

heavier

pesado (más pesado que, el más pesado)

más pesado que

holds less (page 189)

holds less

contiene menos

contiene menos

holds more (page 189)

holds more

contiene más

contiene más

holds the same (page 189)

holds the same

contiene la misma cantidad

contiene la misma cantidad

Glossary/Glosario

English		Español

H

hot (page 193)

caliente

hour hand (page 239)

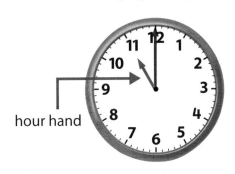

hour hand

manecilla horaria

manecilla horaria

I

in all (page 281)

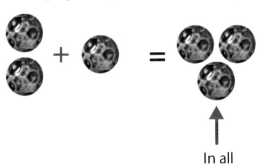

In all

en total

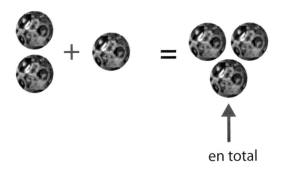

en total

J

join (page 285)

3 birds and 2 birds join.

juntar

Hay 3 aves y se les juntan 2 más.

Glossary/Glosario

English	L	**Español**

length (page 179)

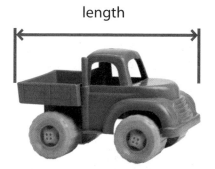

length

longitud

longitud

less than (page 31)

less →

menos

menos →

light (lighter, lightest)
(page 183)

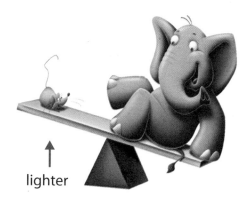

lighter

liviano (más liviano que, el más liviano)

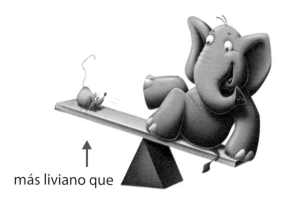

más liviano que

Glossary/Glosario

English	Español

L

long (longer, longest)
(page 179, 181)

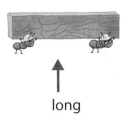

long

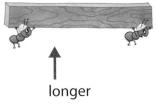

longer

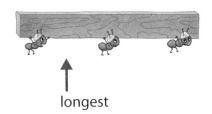

longest

largo (más largo que, el más largo)

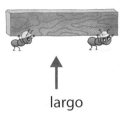

largo

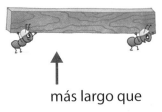

más largo que

el más largo

M

middle (page 73)

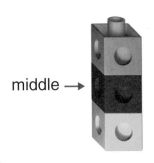

middle →

medio

medio →

minus sign (−) (page 321)

$$5 - 2 = 3$$

minus

signo de menos (−)

$$5 - 2 = 3$$

menos

Glossary/Glosario

English Español

month (page 233)

mes

month

Sunday	Monday	Tuesday	Wednesday	Thursday	Friday	Saturday
		1	2	3	4	5
6	7	8	9	10	11	12
13	14	15	16	17	18	19
20	21	22	23	24	25	26
27	28	29	30			

April

mes

domingo	lunes	martes	miércoles	jueves	viernes	sábado
		1	2	3	4	5
6	7	8	9	10	11	12
13	14	15	16	17	18	19
20	21	22	23	24	25	26
27	28	29	30			

abril

more than (page 29)

más

more than →

más →

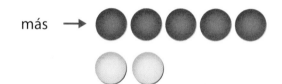

morning (page 229)

mañana

Copyright © Macmillan/McGraw-Hill, a division of The McGraw-Hill Companies, Inc.

Glossary **G13**

Glossary/Glosario

English		Español
number (page 45)	N	**número**

number (page 45)

$$1, 2, 3, 4, 5, 6, 7, 8, 9$$

numbers 1–9

número

$$1, 2, 3, 4, 5, 6, 7, 8, 9$$

numeros 1 al 9

O

o'clock (page 239)

9 o'clock

en punto

9 en punto

order (page 59)

$$1, 3, 6, 7, 9$$

These numbers are in order
from smallest to largest.

orden

$$1, 3, 6, 7, 9$$

Estos números están en orden
del menor al mayor.

ordinal numbers (page 119)

↑   ↑   ↑
first   second   third

número ordinal

↑   ↑   ↑
primero   segundo   tercero

Glossary/Glosario

English		Español
	 **O**	

over (page 71)

over

sobre (arriba)

sobre

 P

pattern (page 77)

A, B, A, B, A, B

patrón

A, B, A, B, A, B

picture graph (page 139)

Our Favorite Toys

gráfica de imágenes

Nuestros juguetes favoritos

plus sign (+) (page 289)

$$5 + 2 = 7$$

↑

plus

signo de más (+)

$$5 + 2 = 7$$

↑

más

Glossary/Glosario

<table>
<tr><th>English</th><th>R</th><th>Español</th></tr>
</table>

real graph (page 133)

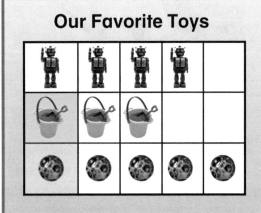

Real graphs have real objects on them.

gráficas reales

Las gráficas reales contienen objetos reales.

rectangle (page 259)

rectángulo

roll (page 257)

rodar

round (page 263)

not round   round

redondo

no redondo   redondo

Glossary/Glosario

English	S	Español

same as (page 179) / el mismo

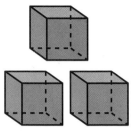 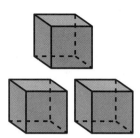

same color, same number

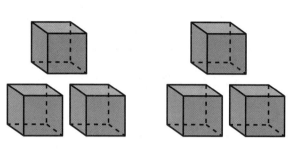

el mismo color, el mismo número

same number (page 27) / el mismo número

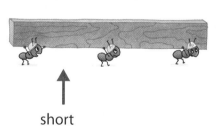
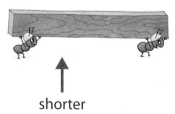
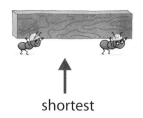

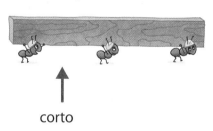

short (shorter, shortest) (page 179, 181) / corto (más corto que, el más corto)

short

shorter

shortest

corto

más corto que

el más corto

Glossary/Glosario

English		Español
	S	

side (page 261)

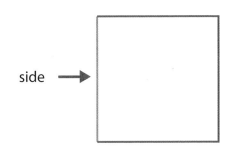

side →

lado

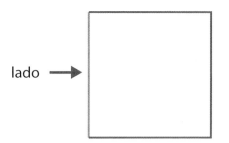

lado →

slide (page 257)

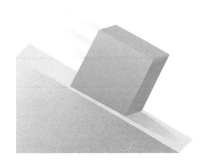

diapositiva

sort (page 19)

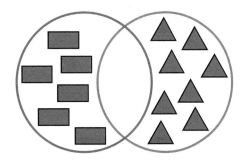

sorted or grouped by shape

ordenar

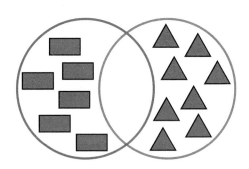

ordenado o agrupado por su forma

sphere (page 255)

 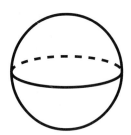

esfera

 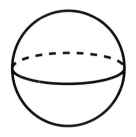

Glossary/Glosario

English	**Español**

square (page 259)

cuadrado

stack (page 257)

pila

subtract (subtraction)
(page 315)

restar (resta)

5 take away 3 is 2. 2 are left.

La resta de 5 menos 3 es 2. Quedan 2.

survey (page 141)

encuesta

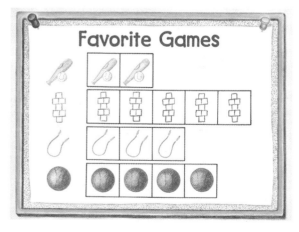

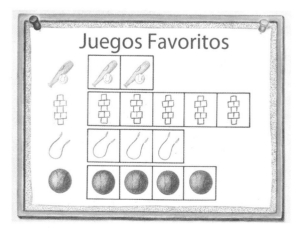

This graph shows the results from a survey.

Esta gráfica muestra los resultados
de una encuesta.

Glossary/Glosario

English	T	**Español**

temperature (page 193)

hot   cold

temperatura

caliente   frio

three-dimensional figure (page 255)

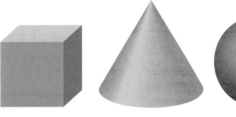 

cube   cone   sphere

figura tridimensional

cubo   cono   esfera

today (page 235)

yesterday   today

Sunday	Monday	Tuesday	Wednesday	Thursday	Friday	Saturday
		1	2	3	4	5
6	7	8	9	10	11	12
13	14	15	16	17	18	19
20	21	22	23	24	25	26
27	28	29	30			

April

hoy

ayer   hoy

domingo	lunes	martes	miércoles	jueves	viernes	sábado
		1	2	3	4	5
6	7	8	9	10	11	12
13	14	15	16	17	18	19
20	21	22	23	24	25	26
27	28	29	30			

abril

Glossary/Glosario

<table>
<tr><th>English</th><th>T</th><th>Español</th></tr>
</table>

tomorrow (page 235)

today   tomorrow

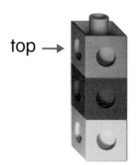

mañana

hoy   mañana

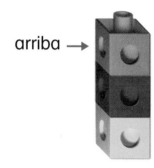

top (page 73)

top →

arriba

arriba →

triangle (page 259)

triángulo

Glossary/Glosario

English		Español
	T	

two-dimensional figure
(page 259)

 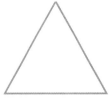

figura plana

	U	

under (page 71)

bajo (debajo)

	W	

week (page 231)

semana

Glossary/Glosario

English Español

weight (page 183)

heavy   light

peso

pesado   liviano

year (page 233)

January						
S	M	T	W	T	F	S
						1
2	3	4	5	6	7	8
9	10	11	12	13	14	15
16	17	18	19	20	21	22
23	24	25	26	27	28	29
30	31					

February						
S	M	T	W	T	F	S
	1	2	3	4	5	
6	7	8	9	10	11	12
13	14	15	16	17	18	19
20	21	22	23	24	25	26
27	28					

March						
S	M	T	W	T	F	S
		1	2	3	4	5
6	7	8	9	10	11	12
13	14	15	16	17	18	19
20	21	22	23	24	25	26
27	28	29	30	31		

April						
S	M	T	W	T	F	S
					1	2
3	4	5	6	7	8	9
10	11	12	13	14	15	16
17	18	19	20	21	22	23
24	25	26	27	28	29	30

May						
S	M	T	W	T	F	S
1	2	3	4	5	6	7
8	9	10	11	12	13	14
15	16	17	18	19	20	21
22	23	24	25	26	27	28
29	30	31				

June						
S	M	T	W	T	F	S
			1	2	3	4
5	6	7	8	9	10	11
12	13	14	15	16	17	18
19	20	21	22	23	24	25
26	27	28	29	30		

July						
S	M	T	W	T	F	S
					1	2
3	4	5	6	7	8	9
10	11	12	13	14	15	16
17	18	19	20	21	22	23
24	25	26	27	28	29	30
31						

August						
S	M	T	W	T	F	S
	1	2	3	4	5	6
7	8	9	10	11	12	13
14	15	16	17	18	19	20
21	22	23	24	25	26	27
28	29	30	31			

September						
S	M	T	W	T	F	S
				1	2	3
4	5	6	7	8	9	10
11	12	13	14	15	16	17
18	19	20	21	22	23	24
25	26	27	28	29	30	

October						
S	M	T	W	T	F	S
						1
2	3	4	5	6	7	8
9	10	11	12	13	14	15
16	17	18	19	20	21	22
23	24	25	26	27	28	29
30	31					

November						
S	M	T	W	T	F	S
		1	2	3	4	5
6	7	8	9	10	11	12
13	14	15	16	17	18	19
20	21	22	23	24	25	26
27	28	29	30			

December						
S	M	T	W	T	F	S
				1	2	3
4	5	6	7	8	9	10
11	12	13	14	15	16	17
18	19	20	21	22	23	24
25	26	27	28	29	30	31

año

enero						
d	l	m	m	j	v	s
						1
2	3	4	5	6	7	8
9	10	11	12	13	14	15
16	17	18	19	20	21	22
23	24	25	26	27	28	29
30	31					

febrero						
d	l	m	m	j	v	s
	1	2	3	4	5	
6	7	8	9	10	11	12
13	14	15	16	17	18	19
20	21	22	23	24	25	26
27	28					

marzo						
d	l	m	m	j	v	s
		1	2	3	4	5
6	7	8	9	10	11	12
13	14	15	16	17	18	19
20	21	22	23	24	25	26
27	28	29	30	31		

abril						
d	l	m	m	j	v	s
					1	2
3	4	5	6	7	8	9
10	11	12	13	14	15	16
17	18	19	20	21	22	23
24	25	26	27	28	29	30

mayo						
d	l	m	m	j	v	s
1	2	3	4	5	6	7
8	9	10	11	12	13	14
15	16	17	18	19	20	21
22	23	24	25	26	27	28
29	30	31				

junio						
d	l	m	m	j	v	s
			1	2	3	4
5	6	7	8	9	10	11
12	13	14	15	16	17	18
19	20	21	22	23	24	25
26	27	28	29	30		

julio						
d	l	m	m	j	v	s
					1	2
3	4	5	6	7	8	9
10	11	12	13	14	15	16
17	18	19	20	21	22	23
24	25	26	27	28	29	30
31						

agosto						
d	l	m	m	j	v	s
	1	2	3	4	5	6
7	8	9	10	11	12	13
14	15	16	17	18	19	20
21	22	23	24	25	26	27
28	29	30	31			

septiembre						
d	l	m	m	j	v	s
				1	2	3
4	5	6	7	8	9	10
11	12	13	14	15	16	17
18	19	20	21	22	23	24
25	26	27	28	29	30	

octubre						
d	l	m	m	j	v	s
						1
2	3	4	5	6	7	8
9	10	11	12	13	14	15
16	17	18	19	20	21	22
23	24	25	26	27	28	29
30	31					

noviembre						
d	l	m	m	j	v	s
		1	2	3	4	5
6	7	8	9	10	11	12
13	14	15	16	17	18	19
20	21	22	23	24	25	26
27	28	29	30			

diciembre						
d	l	m	m	j	v	s
				1	2	3
4	5	6	7	8	9	10
11	12	13	14	15	16	17
18	19	20	21	22	23	24
25	26	27	28	29	30	31

English

Español

Y

yesterday (page 235)

ayer

yesterday   today

Sunday	Monday	Tuesday	Wednesday	Thursday	Friday	Saturday
		1	**2**	**3**	**4**	**5**
6	**7**	**8**	**9**	**10**	**11**	**12**
13	**14**	**15**	**16**	**17**	**18**	**19**
20	**21**	**22**	**23**	**24**	**25**	**26**
27	**28**	**29**	**30**			

April

ayer   hoy

domingo	lunes	martes	miércoles	jueves	viernes	sábado
		1	**2**	**3**	**4**	**5**
6	**7**	**8**	**9**	**10**	**11**	**12**
13	**14**	**15**	**16**	**17**	**18**	**19**
20	**21**	**22**	**23**	**24**	**25**	**26**
27	**28**	**29**	**30**			

abril

Photo Credits

Unless otherwise credited, all currency courtesy of the US Mint.

vi-viii Doug Martin; **I** Ariel Skelley/CORBIS; **2** David M. Dennis/ Animals Animals - Earth Scenes; **3** (tl cl)Stockbyte/Getty Images, (bl bcl)Burke/Triolo Productions/Brand X Pictures/Getty Images, (c)Pat O'Hara/CORBIS, (tc)Goran Kapor/Alamy; **4** (tl)Siede Preis/ Getty Images, (cl)Burke/Triolo Productions/Brand X Pictures/Getty Images, (cr)Getty Images, (tr)joSon/Getty Images, (br)Pat O'Hara/ CORBIS; **5** FAN travelstock/Alamy; **6** Image Source/CORBIS; **7** John Henley/CORBIS; **9** Cory Morse/Getty Images; **11** CORBIS Super RF/Alamy; **13** Randy Lincks; **15** (others)Eclipse Studios, (tl)Brand X Pictures/PunchStock; **16** (bl)Eclipse Studios, (tl)Brand X Pictures/PunchStock; **17** (party hat rabbit cap)IndexOpen, (helmet)Ryan McVay, (fish)G.K. Vikki Hart/Getty Images, (orange)Stockdisc/PunchStock, (pineapple bear)Getty Images, (starfish)Ian Cartwright/Getty Images, (teddy)Getty Images; **18** (plane chair brush)Photos.com, (helicopter)CORBIS, (stool)Getty Images; **25** (tcr)Ryan McVay/Getty Images, (cr)Getty Images, (cl)CORBIS; **27** (drum)Getty Images, (sticks picks)IndexOpen, (bow)Masterfile, (xylophone)C Squared Studios/Getty Images, (Glockenspiel)Chris Stock/Lebrecht/The Image Works; **32** (top to bottom)Stockdisc, CORBIS, Fielding Piepereit, Dave King/ Getty Images, photos.com, Masterfile; **33** (tl)Photos To Go, (cl br)Getty Images, (b)The Stock Asylum, LLC/Alamy, (tr)The McGraw-Hill Companies; **34** (c)Getty Images, (t)Richard Hutchings/ Digital Light Source; **35** (cl bl)Getty Images, (bcl)PhotoLink/Getty Images; **39** F. Lukasseck/Masterfile; **41** (cr br)Eclipse Studios, (bl)Richard Hutchings/Digital Light Source, (tl)The McGraw-Hill Companies; **42** Richard Hutchings/Digital Light Source; **50** (tl)artpartner-images.com/Alamy, (tc)BL Productions/SuperStock, (c bl)photos.com, (bc)super stock; **57** (bird)James Urbach/ SuperStock, (saw)photos.com, (wood)Ted Morrison/SuperStock RF, (hammer)IndexOpen, (nail)Masterfile, (paint)SuperStock RF, (brush)Tony Hutchings/Getty Images, (screw driver)photolibrary. com.pty.ltd/Index Stock, (screw)Leonard Lessin/Peter Arnold, Inc., (birdhouse)Peter Ardito/Index Stock; **58** (hat)Masterfile, (dog)Alison Barnes Martin/Masterfile, (fire hat)IndexOpen, (cowboy hat)Getty Images, (trout)Ron Steiner/Alamy, (pony)G.K. Vikki Hart/Getty Images, (rabbit)PunchStock; **61** (b)Tony Perrottet/Alamy Images, (t)CORBIS; **62** (b)Jochen Sand/Getty Images, (t)Steve Niedorf Photography/Getty Images; **64** (t bl)McGraw-Hill Companies, (cl c)G.K. Vikki Hart/Getty Images, (tcl bl)Getty Images; **67** S Purdy Matthews/Getty Images; **69 70** Eclipse Studios; **81** (others)The McGraw-Hill Companies, (tl)Richard Hutchings/Digital Light Source; **85** (children)Richard Hutchings/Digital Light Source, (maracas)George Doyle/Getty Images, (bell drum guitar)C Squared Studios/Getty Images, (tambourine triangle)Getty Images; **86** (cl)Lebrecht Music and Arts Photo Library/Alamy, (bl bcr)Richard Hutchings/Digital Light Source, (tcl t)C Squared Studios/Getty Images, (tl)Getty Images; **89** (checkers)Jupiterimages, (boots)Digital Vision/Getty Images, (sunglasses)Ingram Publishing/Alamy Images, (flops)Punchstock, (playground)Andrea Rugg/Beateworks/CORBIS, (umbrella)Getty Images; **90** (soccer)Ryan McVay/Getty Images, (kite)C Squared Studios/Getty Images, (paints)Jupiterimages, (bike)CORBIS, (jacks)Getty Images; **91** (bc)CORBIS,

(t)Jupiterimages; **92** (b)The McGraw-Hill Companies, (r)Richard Hutchings/Digital Light Source; **97** Image Source/SuperStock; **98** Getty Images; **99 100** Eclipse Studios; **105** (bag)CSquared Studios/ Getty Images, (others)Mazer; **115** (fish)Ingram Publishing/Alamy, (birds guinea pigs)G.K. & Vikki Hart/Getty Images, (scratching post)Photospin/Imagestate, (seed bell)Mazer Corporation, (fish food)The McGraw-Hill Companies/Jacques Cornell; **116** (wheel)Jason Reed/Getty Images, (bottle collar)Mazer Corporation, (leash)Photospin/Alamy, (mouse)Sergio Piurnatti/ Destinations, (birdcage)Kathleen Finlay/Masterfile, (rawhide)Getty Images; **123** (bl)Getty Images, (tl t)C Squared Studios/Getty Images, (cl)Brand X Pictures/Getty Images; **127** The McGraw-Hill Companies; **129** (bcr b br)Eclipse Studios, (c)The McGraw-Hill Companies; **130** Eclipse Studios; **132** Photodisc Green/Getty Images; **143** (t)Artifacts Images, (bc)Ariel Skelley/CORBIS; **144** (b)Richard Hutchings/Digital Light Source, (t)Bruce Hershey/ Jupiterimages; **146** (c)D. Hurst/Alamy, (tl)Creatas/PunchStock, (bl)C Squared Studios/Getty Images, (b)Getty Images; **149** Raul Touzon/Getty Images; **151 152** Eclipse Studios; **155** (tc)Jupiterimages, (others)photos.com; **156** Masterfile; **157** Ryan McVay/Getty Images; **158 159** Getty Images; **161** (l)Brand X Pictures/PunchStock, (cl)Siede Preis/Getty Images, (cr r)The McGraw-Hill Companies; **162** (l)D. Hurst/Alamy, (cr)Don Farrall/ Getty Images, (cl r)C Squared Studios/Getty Images; **163 164** Stockdisc/PunchStock; **165 166** StudiOhio; **169** (tr)Creatas/ Punchstock, (cl)Robert Glusic/Getty Images, (tc)BananaStock/ PunchStock, (tcl)PhotoLink/Getty Images, (bcr)CORBIS, (tl)MedioImages/Age Fotostock, (r)Richard Hutchings/Digital Light Source, (br)Brand X Pixtures/PunchStock, (bl)Borland/PhotoLink/ Getty Images; **170** Beaconstox/Alamy Images; **172** (boots)Digital Vision/Getty Images, (umbrella)Photos To Go, (sticks)C Squared Studios/Getty Images, (trumpet)Getty Images; **175** CORBIS; **177 178** Eclipse Studios; **183** (t)Richard Hutchings/Digital Light Source, (cl)The McGraw-Hill Companies, (cr br)StudiOhio, (bl)Stockbyte/ PictureQuest, (bcl)Getty Images, (tcl)PhotoLink/Getty Images; **184** (workstation)Photodisc/Getty Images, (ladel)Stockbyte/Getty Images, (bowl)Hemera Technologies/Alamy, (juice jug)Dan Brandenburg/iStockphoto, (bike)CORBIS, (helmet)Comstock Images/Alamy; **189** StudiOhio; **195** (b)CORBIS, (tc)The McGraw-Hill Companies/Jacques Cornell; **196** (bc)Dave King/Getty Images, (t)G. I. Bernard/Photo Researchers, (c)Ingram Publishing/ Superstock, (bl)Jupiterimages; **197** G.K. & Vikki Hart/Getty Images; **198** Photos To Go; **201** Mark Tomalty/Masterfile; **203** Eclipse Studios; **205** C Squared Studios/Photodisc Green/Getty Images; **206** (cl)Photographers Direct, (bl)Masterfile, (tcl)The McGraw-Hill Companies; **218** The Mcgraw-Hill Companies; **219** (bc)David Buffington/Getty Images, (tc)Comstock/PunchStock; **220** (cr)Michael Houghton/StudiOhio, (bc)Cary Anderson/Eagle Eye Pictures/ Photographers Direct; **222** (tl)Karen Whylie/Masterfile, (tcl)Stockdisc/ PunchStock, (cr)Getty Images, (tr)Jupiterimages; **224** Getty Images; **225** Jose Luis Pelaez, Inc./CORBIS; **227** (others)Eclipse Studios, (bl b br)Richard Hutchings/Digital Light Source; **228** Eclipse Studios; **229** (cl)Alamy Images, (bl)Getty Images; **230** (tl)Will & Deni McIntyre/CORBIS, (cl)Mike Powell/Getty Images, (bl)USDA; **237** Bill Bachmann/Index Stock Imagery; **241** Richard Hutchings/Digital

Name _____

Writing Numbers 0 to 5

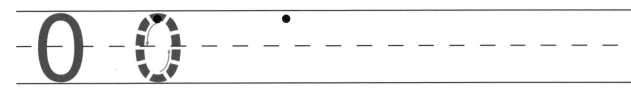

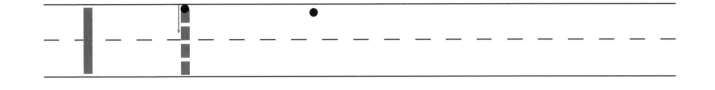

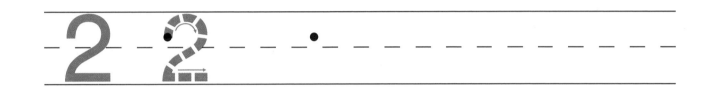

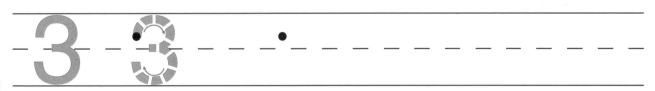

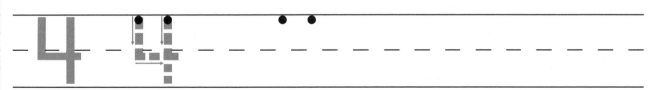

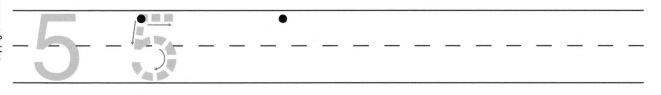

Name _____

Writing Numbers 6 to 10

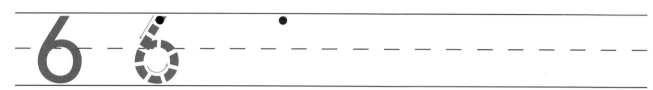

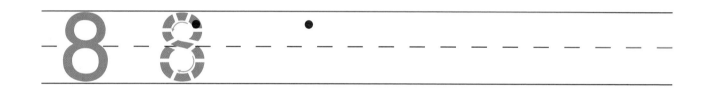

Name _____

Writing Numbers 11 to 15

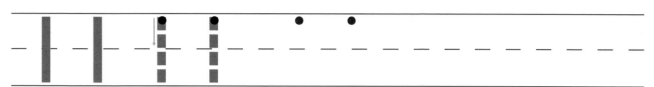

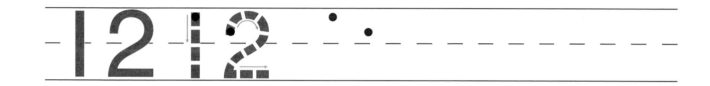

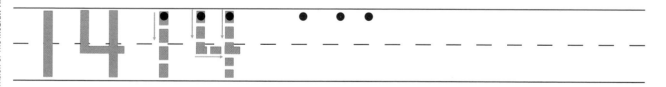

Writing Numbers 16 to 20

16 16

17 17

18 18

19 19

20 20

Writing Numbers

WorkMat I

WorkMat 2

WorkMat 2: Two-Part Mat

WorkMat 3

WorkMat 3: Graphing Mat

WorkMat 4

WorkMat 4: Sorting Mat/T-Chart

WorkMat 5

WorkMat 5: Ten-Frame

WorkMat 6: Ten-Frames

WorkMat 7

Part

Part

Whole

WorkMat 7: Part-Part-Whole

WorkMat 8

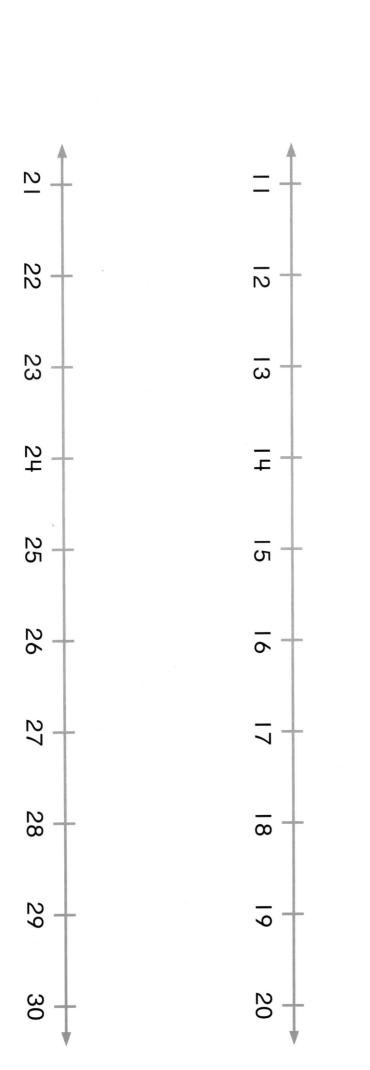

0 1 2 3 4 5 6 7 8 9 10

11 12 13 14 15 16 17 18 19 20

21 22 23 24 25 26 27 28 29 30

WorkMat 8: Number Lines